Until I Met You

Pamela J. Brown

MIDDLE
RIVER
PRESS

Preface

Dearest Arthur Jr. and Richie,

I have created and dedicated my autobiography to you both for the sole purpose of having you understand and get to know PAM vs. MOM. Furthermore, I have written my bio as a tribute to your dad who has displayed the fullest meaning of love in everything he said and did.

Throughout our many years, I have been touched and inspired by the sweet gentleness and kindness that you both learned mostly from your precious dad. You have been blessed by observing the methods he used to function and hold us together as one loving unit. My one fervent prayer is that you will continue to instill your remarkable morals and values into your children through your daily actions.

There is a song titled: "A One in a Million You," sung by Larry Graham. It was our first dance after our wedding vows. Little did I know how literally it would translate into our 40 plus years of marriage harmony! I have fervently tried to let you in to what our very unique chemistry looks like, with the hope that it will serve as a reminder of the substance of our lives together. I'm very proud to say that we are not only in love, we truly like each other—a necessary ingredient in any relationship.

I am confident that you will both continue to shine and be the best you could ever be.

—Your MOM

Acknowledgements

I would be remiss if I didn't convey my sincere gratitude to Rosalee Fyffe and Oslyn McDonald, who have believed in my story from the start of my autobiography journey. I have been encouraged by the sincerity of our family friend Sam Kannan who stayed committed in lending a hand when I needed him. He took time out of his busy day to find a resolve to my questions even though he was not familiar with them. I am also grateful to have received invaluable support and reassurance from my family and close friends during this process.

For my loving and 'cannot do without' husband, I remain appreciative of your patience, understanding, thoughtful gestures and your daily substantial emotional support.

TABLE OF CONTENTS

UNTIL I MET YOU

Humble Beginnings

Mom had my sister and three years later—Me. I know who my father was and met him several times (for maybe thirty minutes)—but alas, I never found my dad. Mom told us that one morning, while she was preparing our porridge, he came home around 7 a.m. after spending the night elsewhere. I was three months old, and she held me in her left arm while she cooked the porridge. My three-year-old sister was sitting on the floor close by. Some heated words were exchanged, he was angrily walking towards her, and she felt like he was going to hit her.

She threw the hot pot of porridge on him with her right hand, picked up my sister and left, with a three-year-old and a three-month-old—never to return. I believe that on that day, her TRUTH found a home in every cell of my three-month-old body. Mom told us that he had previously tried to be physically abusive towards her and she was definitely not allowing that. She did not tolerate any form of domestic violence.

My father lived in a rural town, about a forty-five-minute drive from where we lived. He did not venture out into the city unless it was medically necessary. However, he never once took the time to visit us. About twice a year, Mom sent us on the bus to visit him. These visits only resulted in receiving a few dollars, minus warm loving arms and sweet kisses. Since my father was never present in my life, I have at times wondered if he even loved or cared to see us. Would I ever have had the feeling of comfort with him? Would I have enjoyed his laughter or felt the warmth of love from him? And if he did care, he probably did not know how to articulate those feelings. He may never have received physically expressed loving in his upbringing.

Regrettably, I never had a chance to build a relationship with him to find out who he was, therefore I never felt a tangible connection. Honestly, it may seem callous, but I do not recall ever longing to learn anything about my father. Beyond those visits, I never thought about him nor had any expectations from him.

Thank God, my mom always made me feel like I was wanted, and that I mattered.

Several years later, he had two beautiful daughters and a handsome son—my sisters and brother. He had about eight or nine sisters and brothers. I must say that each time we saw my aunts, uncles, cousins, or grandparents, we were always warmly welcomed and accepted. Through their eyes, there was never a doubt that my sister and I looked exactly like our father and his family.

My DNA

My father was of Portuguese origin mixed with Black. His father (my paternal grandpa) was born on the picturesque island of Dominica. His name was Ishmael. At some point, Grandpa left the island and went to Venezuela. I am not sure why, if he went alone or with his family. My father's mother's family (my paternal grandma) were born in Portugal. Her name was Maria. Because of the civil war in their country, they left Portugal and fled to several countries. After a few years, they were permitted to settle in Venezuela. Grandpa and Grandma met in Venezuela and some years after they were married, they migrated to Trinidad to work in the cocoa fields.

My mom was of Indian descent. Her mom's family were born in India. Many years ago, during the slave trade, Mom's grandfather's family were forced to leave their homeland of India. Due to a labor shortage on the small Caribbean island called Grenada, they were required to work in sugarcane and spice plantations. After many years of demanding, commanding, and rigorous work he was able to earn acres of land as a form of payment. He cleverly cultivated fields of nutmeg, cinnamon and other beloved spices that we all know and love. He invested his profits by planting bananas, papayas, and other tropical fruits.

Mom's grandfather had many children in Grenada with several wives and some of his workers—and he had quite a few! One of his children was my beautiful grandma Agatha. One of the children that Grandma had was my mom. So, it was my great granddad who was born in India.

Back then they never took the time to teach us about our ancestors. I really do not know any more about my DNA than what I have explained. Since those generations are no longer with us, and the family name is pretty much diluted, it probably would be an impossible task to locate any members of my family tree. I have never visited the island of Grenada, but it is most definitely on my bucket list.

I cannot help but wish that I knew about some of the unhappy times, secrets, triumphs, and customs that various members of my family experienced. Or maybe some things are better off not knowing? Despite that, I have always heard that Grenada is such a beautiful island, and I would love to visit it one day.

Accepting What Is

Eight years later, my mom had two additional daughters and a son—my sisters and brother. Throughout my life, I have always referred to all three of my siblings on Mom's side and the three on my father's side as my sisters and brothers. I refuse to acknowledge them in any other way, and I like it like that. It troubles me when I listen to people desperately trying to make huge distinctions when that does not change any of the basic facts. I refuse to try to understand why they do that, because it really does not matter.

My own ideas about the structures of our families changed somewhat as I got older and was able to understand more of their history. Regardless of the truths of each circumstance, I make no judgments. I have learned to accept and embrace what is. I hold no grudges against any of them because life unfolds so differently for each of us. I do not think that revenge or even anger sets you free so why even bother?

I refuse to hold on to the past by making assumptions about what happened with those relationships. It would be very cruel and pointless to even question it. This could have given rise to becoming angry about it all. Over the years, I have understood that anger is like a loaded gun that backfires on the person holding it. It seems to hurt the angry person more than the person they are holding the anger towards. Lugging around anger over time without resolution can one day unintentionally erupt and spew into what may look and feel like volcanic lava.

It is counter-productive to acknowledge and embrace jealousy, hate, and regret. I refuse to engage in futile conversations that dwell on past occurrences. It makes no sense to waste time about happenings that we could do absolutely nothing about.

Years ago, and even today, our families lived their lives with a number of their stories hidden. They were made to feel afraid and ashamed because they had to live up to what the societal and cultural traditions deemed good, fair and acceptable.

I have moved on, accepting what is. I have been focusing on becoming the best I could be in my own life's journey which has been masterful.

THE BEST MOM EVER

Because she was the oldest child, my mom was taken away from school in the third grade to take care of her three younger siblings. Because the adults worked in the fields she had to learn, at an incredibly early age, how to prepare lunch and snacks for her brothers and sister. During those times, it was the custom to do so.

Despite those circumstances, my mother was blessed with natural brain smarts, especially with mathematics. Many years later, I witnessed my mom prepare payroll for a company that had about thirty employees. She accomplished this skillful task without using a calculator or a computer. I watched her create her own spreadsheet where she wrote the date, name, and amount each laborer was paid. She patiently counted the cash, rolling it into a bundle and securing it with a rubber band. I really do not remember how she knew who received which bundle—maybe they were all paid the same amount? How she was able to understand the basic accounting principles was only God's own miracle in motion, given the fact that she was denied the opportunity to secure a proper education by attending the remainder of grades in her school.

Arranged marriages were traditional in Mom's time. They were a dominant and expected part of her ethnic group. Some families "pledged" newborns who grew up knowing about the agreements that were made between the families. When the families deemed that it was time for the young people to marry, they had to comply regardless of their wishes.

When Mom turned 17, her family found a guy who came from a reputable family and who agreed to the marriage. Using her strong opinions, she refused to marry their choice and chose my non-Indian father instead. Consequently, she had to leave her family's home to be with him. This decision caused much grief and disappointment amongst her family. Thus, she became estranged for many years from everyone in her family. She also became an outcast by my grandma—her mother. Sadly, Grandma was forbidden by her family to visit us.

Being a single mom with no family support or education must have been a terrifying experience. When I was around six, my grandma found the courage to step out, walk tall, and visit us. From that day forward she never stopped. Her love, and compassion, was authentic. That component was exactly what my mom needed and longed for. Grandma was proud of us, took care of us and loved us unconditionally. Many years later, Grandma told us that some of the people whom she knew had occasionally tried to encourage her to visit us. However, she was very afraid to go against her family's wishes.

We did not own a car. We either took the bus or walked to places like church, the market, etc. For many years, Mom was on her own working while she lovingly and passionately cared for us. All I know is, she administered financial and every other security possible by simply loving us in every way she could. There were always cooked meals and fresh fruit juice prepared for us. We had daily showers, our hair was combed, and we had a roof over our heads. She was vigilant, never abandoned us and, in her own way, continuously fed our intelligence. Without any doubt, she had this quiet certainty that we had something special to offer all who made it into our life's journey.

In those days, it was not about the nutritional values of the food or whether you wanted to eat what they cooked. It was one meal for everyone. Her generation was more concerned with putting food on the table and clothing us, all the while preparing us to meet the world. Their main concern was keeping us safe. They were all extremely hard workers and never had the conveniences as we know them.

When I became a teenager, I grew in my own imperfect understanding of the depth of the many sacrifices, thought processes, and huge realistic responsibilities required to be a mother and a wife. I will always hold eternal gratitude to our mother for never giving up on us and for the daily caring, training, discipline and ensuring that we were well educated. By her doing so, each of us received a post-secondary education while we developed good citizenship skills.

Growing up without my father, I never, ever felt that I was left behind, was missing out on life or that I was any different from friends who grew up with both their parents. My mom did the best she could while she desperately tried to meet our basic needs with all the tools and knowledge she had at the time. I recall hearing her say that some people had asked her to have us adopted because they saw how tough she was having it. My paternal grandfather told her that people give away their animals, birds, vegetables, etc., but never a child whom you have carried. She told us that this gave her the encouragement, courage, strength, purpose, and determination she needed to continue parenting us on her own.

I would like to think that she dreamed her own dreams while she was playing double duty and had many financial obligations. Unfortunately, she was not able to fulfill her own life's journey. I once asked her if she had any dreams and ambitions. She told me that she had strong ambitions to succeed as an educator. She said that she would have liked to be able to teach math to young people between the ages of 15 and 18. What a loss to our society! Her personal dreams had to be put on hold and sadly never came true.

She used to tell us that a good, sound education was one of those few possessions that no one could take away. She believed that a good education enlightens not only us but the world! Looking back at those days, I know she always had our best interests in mind.

She was desperately alone, strong, afraid, and worried about how she would feed and clothe us. My mom was pure love.

On more than a few occasions I remember her telling us that if we did not learn something new every day, then we have undoubtedly wasted that day! We should always put ourselves in a position where we could daily enhance our knowledge.

Those words have been an undying lantern that never, ever, stopped guiding me in forging ahead with my life. During those growing years, we could not grasp the true and full meaning of what she told us. I am happy to say that I never, ever, forgot the wisdom she taught us.

She was a deeply loving woman who really did not have the time nor the know-how of showing us a lot of physical love. Mom was never a hug-gy-kissy person and no doubt, that came from how she was raised by the generations before her. They did not grow up getting pats on the backs or kisses on the cheeks. Despite it all, they turned out to be incredibly wise and guided us in so many ways.

She taught me this poem when I was around nine years old:

What a little thing am I, hardly higher than the table
I can eat, play, and cry, but to work I am not able.
Nothing in this world I know, but Mama will try to show me
She is so kind I know, sweet Mama I love her so.
Sometimes she puts me on her knees, for her sweet kisses
Oh, how good I will try to be, for such a dear mama as she.

She knew what was important and what she did every day always showed it. There is so much that I could not and still do not even fully understand about how much she had to sacrifice for our family. Or how tiresome it must have been, working long hours as a waitress at a Chinese restaurant only to return home to take care of us.

She focused on helping us build our ability to cope with the ups and downs of life. She equipped us to deal with the mountains and valleys that would be coming our way. Every day she looked after and guided us, worried about us, fed us and loved us deeply without expecting anything in return.

She was a young, beautiful, and clever woman who worked awfully hard at multi-tasking to provide a safe and well-developed life for us. She treasured and was immensely proud of all of us. She must have felt many bouts of frustration and even despair. Yet she never gave less than her best to us. I am sure that every hurdle she faced in life, she hoped and prayed that it would be her last. She never had exciting careers or beautiful clothes. She never had opportunities to experience dining in an upscale restaurant, driving a vehicle, sitting in a fancy car or travelling the world.

One of the experiences I clearly remember is that oftentimes, our hair became infested with head lice which is contagious and spreads very quickly. When one of us got infected, we all became infested. They feed on your blood and lay an egg called a nit which, if left, would hatch and our hair would become even more infested. It is one of the worst feelings when lice crawl around in your head. You can scratch all you want but you cannot stop it.

The only thing Mom said to us was that she was going to the "control board." In those days, the word "why" did not exist in our vocabulary. She returned with a white powder that she mixed into a paste. She parted our hair in small strands and pasted the mixture throughout. Afterwards, she tied our head with a white cloth. This resulted in what seemed like hours of sheer torture. It really was only about 20 minutes, while the lice ran around until they eventually died, YES!

She placed a large wooden barrel in our backyard. She filled it with warm water and picked an assortment of leaves from the trees and vines. She crushed them with her bare hands into small pieces and immersed them in the barrel of water. Back then, they used a lot of the leaves from fruit trees, vines, and plants to either brew tea or use for other medicinal purposes.

I really don't know the benefits, if any, or the purpose of those leaves in relation to the cleansing of our hair, and of course we dared not question it. She washed out that paste from our hair several times whilst we were bent over this barrel and this whole process seemed like hours. When it was all over, our hair was full of those small pieces of leaves and, by the way, the length of our hair extended to our armpits.

Can you even imagine what came next? She had to comb out the hair while trying to remove every leaf. She patiently combed it over and over to remove not only the leaves but the tangles as well. Where was the hair conditioner when we so desperately needed it? Now back then, in the islands, I do not think we knew what hair conditioners were. This was around the late fifties. I am not sure if they were sold in Trinidad and Mom didn't know about it or could not afford to buy it.

My guess is, if they were sold there, they were probably expensive, and she could not afford to buy them or thought it was a waste of her precious money.

Folks, to say that this was an arduous task is the only way that I could describe it. But once again, without complaining she gave us her ALL.

I would like to call this unconditional love of the highest level.

༒

In my early years, I was nurtured by an Indian mother and an Indian grandmother. Because my father was mixed with Portuguese and Black, I find it difficult if not impossible to identify with any one race regardless of what the official agreements deem as legal. I wholeheartedly believe that it really does not matter. More importantly, one should look inside me and examine my values and principles vs judging my outward appearance.

I do not belong wholly to any one race and to choose one of the many races that embody me would be wholly unfair to relinquish the others. I resent and refuse to be a victim of racial exploitations. What difference does it make? I am more than happy, when required, to take my seat in the "other" box.

Because my mom was fully responsible for raising us I could not and would not deny the Indian DNA that is half of my true identity. I will always recognize this part of myself as I do the other parts of my composition.

As much as I have tried to identify with one race, I do not wholly belong anywhere. And that is my TRUTH. I am not lost. Instead, I am fully grounded and wonderfully made.

My Dearest Grandma

My mother's mom (maternal grandma) was born and raised on the lovely island of Grenada. Her father, who was born and raised in India, instilled in her many of the customs he knew. Grandma had her four children in Grenada, and I really do not know how she ended up in Trinidad with her family. My guess is, because the islands were located so close to each other, they moved about quite freely wherever they could find work. This was a long time before work visas and citizenship requirements were enforced. Grandma lived in a small country town and I have fond memories of good times spent at her home during summer and Christmas vacations.

Life in the country had a different vibe. They definitely were not rushed. Everyone seemed tranquil, knew each other, and were always eager to lend a hand to fix what was broken or needed building. There was always a sense of calm and they seemed to appreciate the surrounding beauty. They shared the fruits and vegetables they grew and checked on their neighbors if they did not see them in a while. In those rural areas, most of their homes were built on acres of land. They were able to grow their vegetables and fruits without using chemicals and unnatural substances. It was always a welcome treat to enjoy the bountiful variety of fruits from their thoughtful and unselfish neighbors. Much unlike how we live today.

There was little traffic, and you could hear the sounds of the wind rustling through the trees. You could also hear the bus as it made its stops long before it got to her house.

We were able to pay attention and enjoy the different colors and sounds of the various animals and birds. Unlike city folks, they rarely moved around from one house to another. Generations of the same family were raised in the same house. Today, if you went back to visit those areas and tried to find a family member or friend who you grew up with, you could ask anyone you met, and chances are they would be able to update you on their developments. They were always easy to talk to and were interested in updates in our lives and willing to offer advice or make suggestions to fix a situation.

Even today, many of them still choose not to live in the city and visit only when they need medical attention or to buy items that they were not able to get at their country stores. Their own ideas of busy metropolitan areas and what seem like constant turbulence and chaotic crowds is not the type of lifestyle that appeals to them. The proximity of the houses and high prices of the produce is also a deal breaker for them. Their preference is to live away from all of that.

For hundreds of years, they survived using homegrown remedies that their ancestors understood and used long before our modern medicines existed. It was admirable to observe how they effectively used the barks and roots of many trees. They used various plants such as aloe vera and the Wonder of the World plant that grew in everyone's backyard. Somehow, they discovered that they had healing abilities to cure such ailments as cuts, boils, stomach aches, rashes and even cancer. They were quite content to use those therapeutic methods without ever visiting a doctor. This is another aspect of life that you would never expect in the city.

One of the precious values that my grandma instilled in us related to our behavior and solemn relationships with every book, regardless of the types or genres. Books were meant to be fully and completely respected at all times—no exceptions. She taught us to sleep with a textbook next to our pillow each night. The belief is that knowledge would somehow seep into our brains through the process of osmosis while we slept. We were not allowed to throw them, play with them, hit each other with them, put dogears in the pages, write in them or drop them on the floor. Oooooh that was a serious booboo that resulted in her quarreling with us.

She reminded us that it was an act of gross disrespect and an insult to the books. When we were finished reading a book, she had an exact protocol that we needed to follow. After we closed the book, we had to kiss the cover, touch our forehead, and then touch the top of our heads before putting it away. Grandma was taught this aspect of deep religious and cultural belief by her father whose family were born and raised in India. She believed that nothing could be more important than knowledge from a good education. She passed these values on to us and moved me in such an appealing way that I was able to pass them down to our sons.

She had all types of fruit trees in her yard and of course I was always the one who climbed them to pick the mangoes, oranges, grapefruits, plums, different types of cherries and guavas etc. There was a Brazil nut tree which I think is one of nature's most fascinating trees. This tree is very tall and bears a large wooden pod shaped like a large school bell that hangs downwards. Each pod has a semi-soft center at the bottom. Somehow the bats knew when these nuts were ready and pecked against the center of the hard-shelled pods until the nuts dropped to the ground. There would probably be between twenty and thirty nuts.

When that happened, we screamed in delight when we woke up the next day and saw those Brazil nuts scattered all over the yard. After we gathered them, we placed each nut on a large stone and used a smaller stone to crack open the hard shell. I guarantee you, that if you ever tasted the fresh flavor of a Brazil nut, you would never eat the ones we buy at the store—the flavors are far apart!

During summer holidays, some of our neighborhood friends loved to travel with us on the bus to Grandma's house to catch birds. They usually brought with them bird cages that they had already made as well as extra material to build other cages. They knew the sounds of the various birds and their whistles sounded just like them. In no time, the birds entered the cages and ultimately got caught. It was always a feast for the eyes to take in the natural beauty of the blends of colors in each of them. One of my favorite birds, the sun parakeets, were gloriously made. Their backs were yellow, around their eyes were red, their wings were a mixture of yellow and green and their under-bellies were yellow and red.

My grandma always welcomed them so warmly that they talked about returning even before we left. The bus did not go near where she lived. It dropped us off at the junction. We had to walk to her house about three to five miles along this country road where the houses were very far apart.

We thought nothing of the distance nor the remoteness. It was a very safe environment and none of us ever gave any thought to the possibilities of being kidnapped or any other dangers. We talked, and laughed, on the way to Grandma's and enjoyed some of the fruits that grew in abandoned fields. Not many people owned cars so the few that we saw were taxis.

Those times were filled with so much innocent fun as we watched our friends become so innovative. They built their cages from scratch using whatever materials they could find or afford to buy. We spent most of our days playing in the backyard where there was a long horizontal shed. It was detached from the house and had two large wide hammocks and some benches. Man, with that country island breeze, you could float away in those strong hammocks forever.

Her house had no indoor pipes with running water. One of her sources of water was a well in her backyard just down the hill from her house. If you knew the taste of that water, trust me, you would not drink the water we buy today. The well was not secured by a fence or a wall. We were not allowed to get too close to it because she was afraid that we could fall in. But of course, when she stepped out, we did what most kids would do. We went to the well to fetch small buckets of water just to splash against each other.

She also had several large drums that were used to catch the rainwater. These drums were all strategically placed where they caught the water as it came off the roof. Each drum was covered with a piece of fine mesh. It was tied very tightly with string to keep it in place. It filtered out leaves and other contaminants. That water was always clean. It was used for everything, laundry, showers, watering her plants and for cooking. In those days, island people did not know what hot showers were. Because we did not know the difference, bathing in that rainwater never fazed us.

Grandma cooked on a "fireside" which was molded out of a mixture of mud and straw; water was used to bind it together. It was molded in the shape of a horseshoe with a peak on the top left, center and right, to hold the pots in place. She used dried wood and kerosene to ignite the fire.

She was a devout Christian of the Seventh Day Adventist faith and upheld an extremely strict protocol about the Sabbath. The Sabbath is observed from sunset Friday to sunset Saturday. At the onset of sunset on Fridays, the radio was turned off and all cooking, cleaning, showers, playing and any other type of activities abruptly ended to welcome the Sabbath. To welcome the Sabbath, we had to have our heads covered with a cloth, and at certain intervals we sang hymns. She read her chosen Bible verses, she prayed, then explained those verses that she had just read.

While I observed her during those solemn God moments, I found myself growing even closer to my dear grandma. I deeply felt her sincere, loving, and caring self and I so admired that. I am filled with huge gratitude and respect that she was able to teach us about God during those early years of my life. After welcoming the Sabbath, we were not allowed to talk, but we could read books. If we chose to read, we used kerosene lamps because this rural area had no electricity. Because the sun had already set, it was dark outside, and there were no streetlights and there really was nothing to do. It did not bother us to get to bed early in preparation for the next day.

Every Saturday was a day set aside for all-day church programs. She lived about 30 minutes from the church. We attended every class and every service. We all ate lunch in a communal room where everyone shared what foods they brought. The food was room temperature because heating up any food was considered work and not allowed. Also, microwaves were unheard of back then and even if they had one, they probably would not have used it. These dishes were by no means what we refer to as gourmet, but you tasted the love in every dish. Yes, hot, or cold, it was country food at its finest! Hmmmmm, so good.

Grandma picked cocoa from the fields and had a cocoa house built in the shape of a triangle at the side of her house. The triangle-shaped roof of the cocoa house was supported by wheels that ran on a track much like a train. The roof was pushed back on sunny days, to allow the cocoa pods to be naturally dried by the sun. It was pushed back in place at sundown or if it rained. It was quite a unique and sensible add on to homes in these rural areas. City folks missed out on experiencing this. When the cocoa pods ripened, they were cracked open and the beans inside were spread out to dry in the cocoa house. Once these beans dried out completely, she roasted them in a huge iron pot over a wood fire.

She then began the chore of grinding them in an iron grinder; I think we called it a mill. It was mounted at the edge of her kitchen table. She had to turn it manually until the beans became a fine powder that looked like (but not with the same flavor) other brands of hot cocoa that we buy today. The result was a smooth, aromatic cocoa powder that had the most unforgettable fragrance—my grandma's. Oh, the smell of the whole process was out of this world. It left us longing for her to finish grinding it. The cocoa tea that she made and sweetened with condensed milk was to die for. It was fresh and so flavorful.

Folks, the flavor of her homemade cocoa was such a soothing and welcoming that you never, ever, forgot and that left you wanting more. It is a hearty treat for everyone's weary soul. Today, I am much older and there's no way that I could drink that cocoa tea. I would be sure to fall into a diabetic coma because in those days they used a lot of condensed milk.

Just like the cocoa, she also dried coffee beans in the cocoa house. When the coffee beans were dried, she followed the exact same process by roasting, then grinding them into the finest powder. Even though we were not allowed to drink coffee the fragrance just drove us nuts. Those methods must have been very tedious and painful to her arms and fingers, but you never heard her complain. I guess it had to be done for them to be able to enjoy their own cocoa and coffee so complaining would not have solved anything. The powders looked just like those products we buy today. I do not need to tell you that her coffee was by far more wonderfully made.

I used to marvel at the whole process of how she made cakes and breads from scratch. Blenders and cake mixers were either unheard of or they could not afford them, or they were just nonexistent. Every step was done by her loving hands. When she made her cakes, she added the peel from a fresh lime while beating her eggs—to cut out the freshness. The sugar that she used was dark brown and coarse. Mixing the butter with that sugar by hand was very time consuming and tedious. The butter that she used was salty. Before she blended it with the sugar it had to be "washed out." She added water to the butter and stirred it for what seemed like forever.

She then threw out that water and repeated the same process at least three times. Because I did not and still do not like raisins or currants, she always baked a special small sponge cake (pound cake) just for me. It was always distinctively tasty, making me feel extra special. Many years later, after my father died, I found out from one of my sisters, that he too also disliked raisins—coincidence?

I had the highest regard for her bread making process. After she kneaded the flour with her yeast over and over, she placed it in a bowl. She carefully covered the bowl and tied a string around the rim of the bowl to prevent dirt and other things like insects and leaves to permeate. She took it outside and placed it on a table in the yard to allow the dough to rise by the natural heat from the sun. Once the dough rose, she formed the loaves in her desired shapes and placed them on banana leaves. Banana leaves were washed, dried, and placed over the fire for a few seconds to "soften" them a little. The leaves were put on a tray, then placed in the oven.

Banana leaves were used for baking back then and are still an excellent substitute for aluminum foil. Once again, bread made by her hands was incredibly tasty.

Throughout these very tedious processes I never heard her complain. I guess that is why you could taste so much LOVE when you ate her breads and cakes. Her oven was made from a large empty oil drum skillfully re-designed to be an oven. It was placed in the yard when she needed it. They cut out a "door" in the body of the drum and on the inside, they welded two or three iron shelves. A coal pot full of lighted coals was placed at the bottom of the drum to provide heat underneath. At the very top of the drum, she had a wood fire that she evenly distributed to avoid the bread and cakes from cooking in only one area. She called it "fire on top and fire below." It was so very inventive! Some of the best tasting breads and cakes I have ever tasted came out of her "oil drum" oven. What I would do today to eat from her sweet, loving hands.

When guavas were in season, she took her coal pot out in the yard, lit it up and boiled a huge pot of the ripe guavas for what seemed like hours. After it cooled, she strained them through a thick cloth to get all the skins and seeds out of the liquid. The strained liquid was then returned to the pot and what looked like tons of sugar was added and left to simmer down till it got to the right consistency. After it cooled, she spooned out the jelly into jars and stored them in her larder. The end product was the best tasting guava jelly and when you added some of her jelly on a slice of her bread—true Heaven!

A few years later, while preparing to leave for nursing school, my grandma told me in a very loving and sincere way: "When you go out into your new spaces in the world, make sure you leave them better and more beautiful because you have lived in them." Since I was a mere teenager with my own very vague ideas of what the world was like, I did not understand then, the depth of her thoughts. I would like to think that over the years, I have tried my best to fulfill her profound and superb wish.

Many years later, in 1982, when we travelled back to Trinidad with our two sons, she came to visit us at Mom's house in the city. My grandma caught the bus, carrying with her a large bag of provisions, fruits, Brazil nuts and whatever else she could gather up for us. Where the bus dropped her off, she had to walk about half a mile to get to us. Just like she does in the country where she lived, she arrived with the bag on her head which to me looked heavy. If my grandma was still here, she would still do it her way by walking a half mile or even more just to get to us. My term for that is: Matchless love in the highest order. She welcomed and enjoyed her time with us. We loved and looked forward to those special moments when she called our sons: "my little Americans."

My grandma was incredibly pleased with whom I married and asked us to kneel for her to confer her special blessings on us. She prayed for us in a very distinct way that only she could. During those sacred moments, I opened my soul to her to receive her blessings. Even though I was now an adult, they were truly God moments and meant the world to me. In some special ways, it signified to me that she was to some extent approaching the sad completion of her earth's journey.

Recently I had the opportunity to revisit where her charming light-green house once stood so bold, proud, and welcoming to all. While taking in the concrete pillars and ruins of her once beautiful and inviting home, I honestly did not feel much sadness. Instead of feeling gloomy, a warm, happy, supportive, and very immense blanket of gratitude covered me. My precious memories went into full rewind and allowed me to once again "see" some of those unique, loving, innocent, sweet, and carefree times. She cared so deeply about us and constantly fed us with her morals and values. I stood there "watching" her in her backyard while she washed her long hair that extended down to the top of her buttocks. She would bend over a bucket filled with water while she dipped and poured the water on her hair. When she was done, she used a towel to partially dry it. While she was still bent over, she "beat" the remaining water out of her hair. She put the towel against the middle of her hair and "beat" it in a downward stroke.

It was fascinating and admirable to watch how she handled her beautiful hair. She was not a stylish woman and usually pinned up her hair using a lot of hairpins. In fact, I barely remember seeing her long hair loosely hanging. Yes, I was able to feel a warm, appreciative, and spiritual connection with my grandma. The vibes were real and profound but in no way fearful. I feel so blessed to have experienced life in the country at my grandma's house. My Blessed mom and grandma were like no other moms and grandmas.

THE MARROW OF MY BONES

Some of my fondest childhood memories revolve around the fun times spent with my cousins. We spent many summers and holidays at their home. There was always a lot of movement, activities, and laughter while we were all developing in our own ways under the ever-watchful eyes of my aunty (Ma). Ma was always regarded and respected as our second mom. She cared for us as though we were one of her children. When we visited, my cousins were always accommodating and made us feel at home and like we were one of them.

Because we did not have a telephone—we just showed up. They never knew when we were coming. In the simplicity of those times, that's one of the ways that we managed life with basic humanity and caring for each other. It was the norm that our families and friends always warmly welcomed you, sharing whatever foods, fruits, and vegetables etc. that they had. It worked then—without causing any complications or uneasiness.

During summer vacation time, we could stay up late to enjoy many marvelous times together. It provided balance, connection, and a safe haven. We were grounded and became whole. We played Bingo, Ludo, and other board games for non-monetary prizes. Some were dinner mints, sugar cake, red mango, paradise plum sweetie and Wrigley's chewing gum. These times were always the highlight of our nights where innocent and virtuous times were spent cherishing our togetherness.

Uncle (Pa) was ever the greatest hard-working provider. Since he had a large household, he worked tirelessly. He was always gone before the sun came up and returned late at night. Pa owned a Chinese restaurant in the heart of the town where they lived. My Pa was an entrepreneur from his youth, running businesses and working relentlessly to care for his family whom he loved very much. In addition to his restaurant, he had a farm where he cultivated various fruits and vegetables.

He owned a black jitney and removed the back door of it to sell the seasonal produce. He harvested watermelons, oranges, plums, and many different types of vegetables. When it was time to sell them, he drove around several neighborhoods and when he blew the horn of the jitney, people came out of their homes to buy his produce. They all knew him, and it was a very good way to sell your local products thus providing a steady source of income.

The older sons were groomed to assist Pa by working in their Chinese restaurant. This allowed them to hone the craft that resulted in a lucrative livelihood for several of them many years later. They have all moved on with their lives and have become successful, mostly in the food industry. I sense that the skills they attained by working in the restaurant gave them that vital head start in the business.

The daughters were at home under the watchful eyes of Ma. One of the things that amazed me was how the older siblings were taught to be responsible for the younger ones. They cared for them almost as if they were their own children. They cooked, did the laundry, and cleaned the house as though it was theirs—no excuses. Ma would not hear of it. Without realizing it, they were being skillfully prepared for their adult life.

The girls have all had productive careers and are thriving with their families balancing all that life throws at them. Most of them live in one state which makes it amazingly easy to celebrate family occasions. Over the many years, we have gone to the weddings, birthdays, funerals, etc., to enjoy their great company and update each other about our lives. They have been, and still are, an integral part of my foundation. They are my blood, the very marrow of my bones, and are a part of my landscape. This fact, I cannot/would not deny or escape.

Elementary School

In the third grade, I was lucky to be chosen to play Snow White in our end of year school play. It felt really cool to play such a major role. The magic and delight of that beloved classic with so many memorable musical pieces are unforgettable. I still like humming this song: "Hi ho, hi ho…" The dwarfs were the cutest ever. Mom sewed my blue blouse and yellow skirt. She combed my hair in two braids and at the end of them, she added red ribbons. She had a Singer machine and sewed all our clothes which traditionally was what most people did back then. I really don't remember her buying clothes for us already made from a store.

In the fifth grade, Mr. Peters was my school icon—even though I feared him, and I think we all did. School started at 9 but we had to be seated in his class at 8:30 for spelling drills. We knew the sound of his car and once we heard it, we all hurried to our seats to await his half-hour spelling lesson of the day. He was stern, wise, firm, and kept an eagle eye on us. He sat at his desk with his first and second fingers pressed up against his temple while he called out the words for us to write down in our notebooks. All the while, repeating several times without even looking up, "speed and accuracy." He was a no-nonsense and authoritative type of teacher who thankfully demanded nothing but excellence from every student.

I have to say that one of my best writing skills is spelling and as you read my autobiography, Mr. Peters is all over it. He was experienced, clever and extremely knowledgeable of his profession. Unfortunately, I never thought of returning home to personally thank him for covering me with such a valuable attribute. I truly regret this because he was so deserving of receiving my gratitude. I got busy with my own life and just never thought about it until later in my life and it was too late then.

During the fifth grade, every student who reached the age of eleven had to take this national test called the 11-Plus exam. The results of this exam determined which high school we attended. We had to complete an application by indicating the names of the three high schools we wished to attend by indicating our first, second, and third choices. Naturally, we all indicated the top schools that were highly rated. We did not consider how far away these schools were even if we lived close to the local high school, it did not matter. We just wanted to attend the best schools. If you scored high in the exam, you were sent to the best schools which were our first and second choices. Some of us—me—had to travel "out of town" to attend a school which was very highly rated.

Every Friday, before our classes ended, we had recess from 2 to 3:30. From the moment the school bell rang at 2 o'clock, I would hustle out to the field and play without ceasing until that bell rang again for dismissal at 3:30! Most times, whilst playing, I took off my shoes and socks to either climb the trees or just run wild—yes, I was a bit of a wild child. Consequently, when it was time to leave, I could not remember or find the shoes and socks and would have to end up going home without them.

Now try to picture this—I have no shoes or socks, my hair has come all loose from my braids, my face all flushed and sweaty, the uniform blouse loosely hanging, just looking one hot mess—I got licks some Friday afternoons after school. Sadly, mom had to find the money to go to the store on Saturday to replenish what I had just lost. As an adult, it grieves me when I think of how selfish my behavior was back then. In these early days I was quite a tom boy. I just loved climbing up any kind of trees and rather than climb down, I would jump down from them. Nails and splinters were common happenings on my body, especially my feet.

I loved the game of pitching marbles and was particularly good at it. We would take a stick, draw a large ring in the dirt yard, scatter about a dozen marbles in it and take turns to pitch the marbles out of the ring. The winner was the one who knocked out the most marbles. I also loved dancing the hula hoop. I twirled the hoop around my neck, waist, and arms. Other games I loved were hopscotch, moral, skipping rope and a game called jacks.

In the first grade, a large family of mostly boys moved into the house directly opposite us. There was one girl who was my age, around 6. We instantly became close friends, and we were happy to be in the same class. On many occasions, her parents took me on trips with them as though I was part of their family. After living there for a few years, sadly they had to move to a different town, and we did not see much of each other.

In February 1982 we visited Trinidad and I saw her for the first time in many years. Several years later, she moved to South Florida and we moved there March 1989, but we did not know of our respective moves. Many years later, we were at a party in Miami, and I saw one of her older brothers. After so many years, he was taken by surprise when he saw me and was overwhelmed with excitement and joy. He immediately took me to the back of the room where his sister was. We reconnected in an instant! It was as though we were never separated. Currently, we live about thirty minutes away and I am happy to say that our friendship has not skipped a beat; we continue to live like sisters.

When I was around eleven, my female hormones became alive, and I began getting distracted by boys. Thank goodness, we were not allowed to attend any Carnivals, parties, movies, hang out with friends and absolutely no boyfriends. My few and limited Carnival experiences were looking out the front window at the masqueraders passing by to join up with their respective bands. We were not able to be in the front yard if we wanted to see anything relating to Carnival, it had to be from the front window.

Mom was tough and kept us well disciplined. Mom made sure of it while continuing to monitor our every move—especially me. You dared not question her motives and direction; you just had to do it. Oh yeah, she ran a very tight ship! Life was all about school, church, and home. I understand now why she had to really keep her fingers and toes on me. Due to those raging hormones, I was the most adventurous and would have gone down some troublesome paths! She had to use every bit of her innermost convictions to guide me even when I could not comprehend the decisions she made. I surely did not understand then that yesterday's decisions might end up being tomorrow's realities. Today, I am a miracle in motion because I have this innermost peace about my life!

Sweet Trinidad

I grew up in a charming country that was racially mixed. We were a conglomeration of every race and ethnic group you would ever encounter. We were faintly aware of the differences only because of the various shades of our skin color and the texture of our hair. It just did not matter to any of us; we very simply did not care. In school, one of my best friends had green eyes and brown hair but I never "saw" her that way. I saw her as a good person, and I was extremely comfortable spending my time with her in and out of school.

The adults allowed us to bond freely with their children. No one ever showed any racial or hatred actions to our neighbors because they looked different from us. The neighbors looked out for us as though we belonged to them and took care of us if we fell or when they knew it was time for us to go home. They kept an eye on us and if they happened to see us messing around with guys inappropriately our families were sure to hear about it. For me, I would have been deathly afraid to get "out of line" because word was going to get to my mom, and I would suffer the consequences.

We visited their homes, ate with them, respected their cultural and religious differences, and came away with a deep sense of total acceptance and the knowledge that this is the way our life is supposed to be. This stupid and nonsensical race war that seems to be enveloping many of our households today was not a part of our makeup. It only gives rise to hatred, discrimination, and in some cases violence. It is needless, so wrong, and for what gain? I feel proud, fortunate, and blessed to have been raised in such an unbiased and non-judgmental environment. It was a great time to grow up without needlessly classifying others.

Without a doubt, I believe that we got it right!

Why should we be relentlessly classifying people? It served no purpose then, it makes no sense today, and it should not even be an issue for discussion in our world today. End of story—PERIOD!!!!

We need to find ways within ourselves to absolve every pre-conceived and unfounded notion that we conjure up when we see someone who looks, speaks, acts, or dress in ways that are different from us.

HIGH SCHOOL

My high school education was at a Catholic convent. It was really an awesome educational turning point for me. Our school was originally a boarding school that was run by nuns before it became a public high school that provided free education for all. It had a very high percentage of Caucasians who were born there because their parents were from countries such as America, Canada, and England. Their population at my school was probably around seventy percent! Those of us who were non-Caucasians never even cared and none of us felt that we were any better than the other. Our beautiful island produced oil and it was a huge lure for investors and workers from other countries who either brought their children with them or gave birth to them there. After many years of working there, some of them chose not to return to their countries and remained in Trinidad. Their children attended the boarding school and automatically fed into the high school grades. One of the amazing things is, you may meet someone who looks "white." But when they speak, that Trini accent would be a shocking thing to hear coming out of a Caucasian's mouth.

The interesting thing about this is that even though they looked "different" with hazel, blue, and green eyes, we did not "know" that they were different because racism was not a thing that we knew. That white/Indian/Black/Chinese girl/boy was never part of our vocabulary, thoughts, or conversations. The very thought of us uttering racial slurs were never ever part of our conversations. We all blended in during school activities and never distinguished ourselves in such a way that we did not play games or gather socially in school or in the neighborhood.

With the exception of two, the nuns were all Irish, English, Welsh and Scottish. Our education was of a highly recognized and International standard. School was all about sound academics, proper etiquette, and of course, appropriate conduct. We were taught how to set a table for a meal, how to sit properly at the table, how to hold the cutlery and how to properly excuse yourself when you were ready to leave the table after your meal.

Each morning before our classes began, we had to attend roll call by lining up on the tennis court. Our uniforms were white blouses and blue pleated skirts. It was mandatory that we wore a white lacy camisole or an undershirt under the blouse so that the bra did not show.

The Prefect (class captain) had to walk along the line to take attendance and inspect our uniforms for compliance. Sometimes she was unable to determine whether we complied and could go behind us to press lightly against our blouse. If we were negligent by not wearing an undershirt or camisole, we received one point in conduct against us.

We were being trained to not fall prey to earthliness and worldly desires. In PE classes we were taught Scottish, English, and Irish dances such as the jig. We were also taught rugby and lawn tennis. The nuns and female teachers (there were no male students or teachers) were deeply knowledgeable and experienced but boy were they strict! However, I am not sure if our self-esteem was ever a concern to them.

In our home economics classes, we were taught Scottish and English dishes such as shepherd's pie, bangers and beans, Yorkshire pudding and haggis. One of my favorite dishes that they taught us was a Greek dish called moussaka. We were taught very little of our tasty local cuisine, maybe because they were not familiar with it. Also, in home economics class, we were taught how to use cut-out patterns to cut fabrics and sew items of clothing. I think that their notion was to mold us into an all-round person capable of being the best citizens ever. I will forever be grateful to those nuns for my eminent secondary education.

Every day, we had our religious knowledge class during the second period. We all knew when the nun was approaching the classroom because we could hear the sounds of her rosary beads as they bounced against her thigh. We then rushed to our seats before she entered the classroom.

It was mandatory that we were all seated quietly awaiting the start of our lesson for that day. At the beginning of each class, we had to stand when the teacher entered the room. At the end of the period, when she stood up to leave the class, we had to stand up once again until she left the room. When she began to erase what she wrote on the blackboard, any one of us had to volunteer to do so.

Usually, our homework was to memorize selected verses of the books of the New Testament and recite them verbatim when called upon during class. If you forgot the verses or simply did not memorize them, the punishment was to stand at the back of the class without your book during the entire period. It was an intimidating and scary way to teach us, but I guess they did the best they could.

At the end of each school year, our school held an Academic/Conduct Roll Call. We assembled in the great hall and all the teachers, nuns, and the parish priest took their seats on the stage. If you had an A+ grade, they called out your name along with the subject and you had to go up to the front of the hall and stand on the right side. If you had an F grade, you had to go up to the front to the left side. There were always moments of silence while every teacher looked fiercely at us particularly if you were on the left side. I guess their concept of urging us to better ourselves was through intimidation and humiliation.

I still do not agree with some of their techniques, but I do know that they seemed to have our best interests at heart, and it was their prescribed code of teaching. One day during assembly, our Mother Superior (the head nun) stomped her way down from the stage. The steps were wooden and back then the shoes that the nuns wore were called brogues. The sound of those hard shoes really sounded like stomps.

She grabbed one of my friends by her hair and literally "dragged" her up the steps to the stage and made her face the entire school.

There was a hair product called a relaxer that was used to straighten curly hair. When used regularly and being in the islands, your hair was always exposed to the sun; it caused the hair to turn red. She ridiculed this young lady in front of everyone, teachers, nuns, and the parish priest. She berated her about choosing to become worldly by using such foolish items that would lead us to the devil instead of God. Even though she wanted us to learn from it, I believe wholeheartedly that her method of demonstrating what she deemed as worldly was wrong.

I wish I knew how this incident impacted my friend psychologically then and now. The interesting thing is, I have never forgotten it, so I know for sure that she has not.

On two occasions, they took us on a field trip to watch a movie. That was a huge deal for me since mom never allowed us to go to the movies. I was filled with immense joy and high expectations, even though they were biblically themed movies such as Moses, The Ten Commandments, Ben-Hur, and Golgotha. They were enjoyable and I welcomed the experience of going to a movie theatre. We were all very surprised when they took us to see The Sound of Music because it had a few romantic scenes in it. This movie has turned out to be one of my favorite movies. I am not sure why we never got to go to the movies anymore. I sense that a student either misbehaved or probably disappeared during the movie.

The male high school was located one block before our school. Every day we had to walk past their school before we got to ours! They were not allowed to talk to us. They would get into trouble as would we. Their school was fenced off by a chain link fence. Occasionally, some of them would dare to come close to the fence to whistle at us or to try to pass a note through the fence for a girl they fancied. We were afraid to look over at them so keeping our heads turned away was nothing short of a daily challenge as you could well imagine. At least three times a week we had to leave our school to walk down to the Catholic church for Mass at 11 a.m. and return to church again at 3 p.m. for Benediction. Walking down that hill (next to the boys' school) so many times was sheer punishment!

Once a year, we had a retreat day. On those days, there were no classes—only debates, attending church services and basically spending the entire day in silence, prayer, and solitude. As you can imagine, this was not fun at all. If you were Catholic, you dared not miss school. All other religious groups were exempt from attending school on those retreat days. Talking and laughing was an absolute no-no!

We had to engage in tranquil and solitary reflection. If we were caught, we ended up in detention. In detention, they wrote a long sentence on the board and we had to write it again and again around 500 times. In my final year of school, they decided to hold a sports event by competing against different grades to showcase some of the different sports we learned. It was an exciting concept for us to have some fun playing against each other.

However, the number one rule was moms, sisters, aunts, and female cousins could attend but no male friends or family members such as dads, brothers, uncles, male cousins etc. could attend. Some of the local high school guys decided to break the rule and checked us out from the surrounding rooftops and trees. During many of the events, they whistled, and clapped. Our nuns were not having this, and the event died an early death.

FITTING IN

I did not have the fancy lunches that some of my classmates had or had any money to buy lunch from the cute little Tuck shop on our school grounds. Mom used whatever she had to pack a lunch in my lunch box. I most definitely could not attend football games, dances, movies, and other social events. My mom could not afford those things and quite frankly she focused on protecting us from teenage temptations.

I sometimes overheard classmates talking about meeting up at the Inter-Collegiate games between the various male high schools that had football teams. It was a great opportunity to either find one or meet up with your boyfriend. I don't need to tell you that I never got to experience those events. Mom was not about to let her guard down by giving way to such temptations and for that I am eternally grateful. I would often listen to my classmates plan parties and other after school events just wishing that I could go. Sometimes I felt like I was somewhere I was not supposed to be, almost like I did not fit in. Being a teenager, we are all subconsciously striving to "fit" in, and it really didn't feel good.

I can recall only one occasion when I was permitted to attend a party at my friend's house but there was a certain protocol that we had to follow. Her mom had to ask my mom's permission and the agreement was that I would be able to sleep there—there was no chance of walking home after dark. Also, at this party, the aunties, moms, and uncles sat right there in the very room where we danced! Yes, they were most present and attentive to our every move.

I sure wish that life could once again be as innocent as those times because it was such a pure and harmonious environment that we thrived in and I am so proud to say that I am a product of that era.

Today, I wish that I could find some of my classmates to laugh as we reminisce about it all. Logistically it is almost an impossible task because we have migrated to countries all over the world.

During those growing years, there were several grey patches of things that happened in my life, but I have come to realize that some circumstances that occur are not meant to be understood. Over the many years, I have learned to embrace and accept those unknowns as a normal part of my life because they have nourished my soul in one way or another. Even today I still do not fully understand quite a few things—but it's all good. I firmly believe that people try to do the best they can based on the cards they are dealt.

Many years later, I took my husband with me to visit my high school. One very surprising element was the presence of a security guard at the gate. Because we did not have an appointment, we were not allowed to enter. This security requirement reflects how much our world has changed since I attended school there. I never knew or even thought that an appointment would be a requirement.

While we were walking around the outskirts of the school, we saw one of the teachers in the corridor. As soon as I called out to her and explained our presence, we were immediately allowed to enter. Our school always had beautifully landscaped grounds with rose gardens in several different locations. Those roses were always in bloom and set a sweet and elegant tone for our school environment. The hedges were always trimmed, nicely shaped, and neatly cut back. We were introduced to the school principal who happened to be one of my former teachers. She remembered my name but of course—not the body! I wish that I could say that I remember her, but unfortunately, other than her name, I still don't.

She showed immense pride and excitement. She told us that she was deeply honored that a former graduate who had lived abroad for so long, still took the time to return to visit the school. She proudly walked us both around the entire school and even interrupted some of the classes to introduce me as a former student. I must say that I was absolutely surprised that there were two male teachers as well as a sprinkling of male students but only in the upper-level classes—oh boy!—I was denied that experience but maybe that was for my own benefit. The only "sad" note that I had about our visit was when we got to the chemistry lab. There was a class in progress, but I did notice that some of the equipment like the beakers and funnels seemed a little outdated. I did observe though that every student including the teacher were all wearing lab coats.

In so many ways, I was touched, proud, and most impressed by the visit. I felt engulfed by the truth of having walked those beautiful light-grey terrazzo hallways so many times. She assured me that the high level of education remained at the same standard that I had. My beautiful school looked well maintained and did not at all look dilapidated and aged. My husband was most impressed and touched by what he saw and heard during our visit. When we left the school grounds, he had to pause for a minute or so to wipe off just a tear or two. He was able to get a better sense of appreciation of my culture and was able to further understand where I came from.

My Illness

When I was around twelve, I was diagnosed with juvenile rheumatoid arthritis (JRA)—an inflammatory disease. The joints in my fingers, toes, knees, hips, and shoulders were always swollen and painful. I was unable to wear shoes—only flip-flops. I could not make a fist or hold anything in my hand because the joints were always swollen and warm to the touch. Since my shoulders took a big hit, I was unable to help with chores such as cooking, ironing, and house cleaning. As the disease progressed, I was not able to walk. I quickly got used to moving around by scooting on my butt. I had pretty much become an invalid. Everyday tasks such as feeding myself, taking showers, combing my hair, etc., were so out of the question. And guess who had to help me—my devoted mother.

Because of this disease I was hospitalized over a dozen times resulting in copious school absences. The litany of specialists and constant doctor's visits required to rally round my treatment must have been super overwhelming! How my mother balanced work and taking care of my younger siblings is still a deep mystery to me. Mom had to catch the bus for her visits, travelling about 30 miles each way. She was not able to stay very long with me because she had to either ask a neighbor or some friend to watch my other siblings. Coping with the many trips to the hospital for so many months to visit me while she tried her best to focus on my needs, had to cost a bunch of money, stress, and time. I would not be here today if it were not for God's grace and the due diligence and strength of my mother's love.

I distinctly remember being in a secluded area with two other girls who were around my age. These girls had JRA like me, and their swollen joints were enlarged like mine. None of us were able to walk. One of them used to lie in her bed curled up in a ball; she seemed to be in a more advanced stage than I was. I do sometimes wonder whatever became of them.

During this time too, in addition to my arthritis, my throat was constantly inflamed and painful. Swallowing regular foods was very agonizing and almost impossible to do. I was diagnosed with tonsillitis; my tonsils had to be removed as soon as possible. Since the focus was finding the appropriate treatment for the JRA, the surgery had to wait. Until then, I had to survive on throat lozenges, mashed potatoes, ice cream, juice, and Jell-O. Since that time, I have refused to eat Jell-O! After numerous tests and what seemed like endless visits from many teams of residents and doctors, after a year or so, I felt no relief from my daily aggravated joints.

That dreaded day came when the doctor told my mom what no parent wants to hear: "Take her home and give her whatever she asks for." I can still hear the soft sounds of her cries some nights while she lay in her bed deeply afraid of the inevitable. Financially she was not able to get me additional help from private specialists. She must have been at a loss trying to figure this all out on her own.

Grandma visited when she could and was saddened when she saw my physical condition deteriorating. One day she told me this story that her father (my great-grandpa), had told her many years ago. "There was a young man who was ill and was expected to die. Outside his window, there was a mango tree that was shedding its leaves. He told his father that when the last leaf fell, that would be the day that he died. His father climbed the tree and nailed one of the leaves to the tree ensuring that it would never fall. Each day when he saw that one leaf, he was able to strengthen his will to survive." That young man was her father (my great-grandpa).

Pa and his wife (Ma) showed up one day while I was sitting on the floor. He scooped me up in his arms and took me to their home. Almost every day he took me to numerous doctors, therapists, churches, even a "witch doctor." Pa took me anywhere that he heard about, seeking relief for me from this progressive disease. His commitment and persistence helping us find a cure or relief from my pain was truly admirable, constant, and never ending and for that I have always been eternally grateful.

By then, I was almost thirteen and weighed fifty-two pounds. I experienced severe pains in my joints, and I could see and feel the warmth of the swelling. My fingers and toes were bent to the side and stiff. I knew that it was worsening all over my body. My circulatory, skeletal, and other systemic systems were failing.

Honestly, I do not remember when, how, or even where I was when the miracle happened. Somehow some measure of healing and strength occurred that altered the outcome of my prognosis.

Because I missed so many days from school, I was held back one grade because I needed to fulfill the exact requirements of the syllabus. After an extra year, I was able to graduate! Our graduation carried a precise and strict protocol that had to be exactly as the nuns wished. Only dresses were allowed, and they had to be white, and the length had to cover our ankles. The neck had to be round and cut close to the neck. It had to have sleeves that were either short or long and we needed elbow-length white gloves. By some miracle, we could have a male escort—YES! I did not have a boyfriend; my escort turned out to be my very handsome cousin.

❧

After my graduation, I needed to move on with my life by getting a post secondary education. Mom went to the local high school principal and asked for recommendations of nursing schools in England.

During the lengthy application process, she did not want me sitting idly at home. She signed me up to attend a technical school to learn accounting, shorthand, and typing. The school was located about four houses from my mom's "Mom and Pop" shop. Back then we called it a Parlor.

This school was owned by a guy in his late thirties or maybe even forties. This dude was ambitiously fierce, driven, and ruled the roost in the most aggressive way that came off as mean. When he taught, he not only stood at the front of the class, but he continuously walked around the room to constantly check our work. If it was his intent to intimidate or bully us, he succeeded because his classes were no walk in the park.

After I got home one day, my mom lit into me like a lightning bolt. She went on and on about the fact that she sent me to the school to enhance my education and not for guys. Honestly, I hadn't a clue what she was referring to, but I knew better than to question her. Back then we certainly did not dare talk back to our parents or elders.

We grew up in a time when one of the basic ideas was—do not ask questions, do what you are supposed to do and believe what you are supposed to believe. The adults were to be totally respected at all times, especially teachers, priests, etc. We were cultivating moral disciplines, mindfulness, wisdom, values, and ultimate compassion.

I found out later, that while I was in class, this guy who owned the school, went to her shop, and asked for my hand in marriage! Folks, he never once approached me unless I was so naïve that I simply did not catch on that he was interested in me. Yes, you guessed it—that was my last day at his school. She stopped me from ever going back there. Her decision was fine with me because I did not like him, and marriage was the furthest thing on my mind. I was only seventeen and a half. I was not meant to be an accountant or secretary anyway.

The Ties That Bind

Ten years after I was born, another sister came along. Her dad's (my stepdad) brother and his wife had no biological children. They adopted a beautiful baby girl who became our "cousin." Growing up in the islands, respect for adults was of the utmost, and simply put—mandatory. Everyone became uncle, aunty, cousin, etc. You dared not address an adult by their first name. Whenever my stepdad visited his brother, we all had to go to visit "uncle, aunty and our cousin." She was my age and instantly I really liked her, we became good friends, and I always looked forward to visiting them. It never mattered to us that we were not blood kin. We just accepted each other, referred to each other as "cousin," and still do.

Years later, I went to London and she to New York. Once again, it was not the age of cellphones, so we had no idea of each other's whereabouts. Not long after I got to the U.S., my mom updated me on where she was, and I was able to get her phone number.

Maybe six to eight months later, she brought her beautiful family to our home in Virginia. We were able to renew our wonderful and special friendship as though we had always been together over those many years! We spent an awesome week together bonding and enjoying so many special moments. We spent the entire weekend touring and soaking in so much of the history of Washington, D.C. Naturally, our children called her, and her husband "aunty" and "uncle" and their children became our son's "cousins." Several years later, I told her that we were planning to move to Florida. She was overjoyed and told me that we would have to meet up with her brother and his family. They lived about a half hour away from where we would be living.

We moved to Florida in March and a few months later in August, she and her family visited and stayed with us. During her visit one Sunday afternoon, her brother, his wife and their three children visited our home.

It was a superb evening. We delighted in each other's company with music, food, and swimming. It was pleasing to watch all the kids while they smoothly intermingled. Mine, hers, and her brother's. By the end of that terrific evening, it was clear that our friendship with her brother's family was sealed. Throughout the many years that followed, we grew awfully close to her brother's family. We visited each other's homes, attended various parties together, and shared this common and incredibly significant bond. Somehow, it felt as though we were always family.

When our younger son graduated from high school, we celebrated by hosting a huge party. Naturally, my "cousin's" brother and his family came. By the end of that night, it was evident that a relationship was about to flourish between their youngest daughter and our oldest son Arthur Jr.

He was already in college and she was heading into her senior year of high school. They instantly began dating. The following year, he took her to her prom and shortly after, she began her college education at the same school that Arthur Jr. was attending. Thankfully for all of us, we knew each other's families very well. It was a very pleasing and approved thing to watch their courtship moving seamlessly in one direction. After they both graduated with their bachelor's degree, they were able to secure reputable jobs, bought their house, and one year later in 2008 got married.

That "cousin" whom I met so many years ago when we were both mere teenagers, was contributory in bringing their lives together when she introduced us to her brother's family.

Our son's wife (Arthur Jr.'s) is my "cousin's" niece.

New Horizons

After several months of corresponding to hospitals in England, I was accepted into the registered nurse (RN) program. I would be attending a nursing school that specialized in psychiatric nursing. This school was in a suburban town called Haywards Heath located in West Sussex, England. Mom did not have the money to get my airfare and borrowed the funds from my girlfriend's dad who willingly and without any hesitation helped us out. The night before I left for London, mom held a farewell party to allow friends and family to wish me well for this journey that I was about to undertake. One of our neighbors, who was probably in her seventies, wrote these wonderful words of wisdom in a card and handed it to me.

"Your future lies before you, like a path of untrodden snow

Be careful how you step on it cause every step will show"

To this day I have never forgotten those profound words that have helped guide me in my journey and are still so relative in our world today. I still believe that those words should be one of life's mantras. It has so much depth to it and would light the way for our youth today. When we are young, we do not have the wisdom to understand how our irresponsible choices could one day become a hindrance to our success.

A few days before I left, my mom referred to the clothes pegs that she used to hang out our laundry. She said that each one of them were like minefields that I would weather throughout my life's journey. So off I went to get my RN degree in psychiatry. I must tell you that I was incredibly happy and excited to be away from home. I felt so inhibited and sheltered and I wholeheartedly knew that I needed to break free taking all that they gave me and making the best of it.

Like most teenagers, I so wanted and needed to bust loose and experience some of those young adult freedoms like partying, having a boyfriend or hanging out late with my friends!

COLLEGE

I arrived in London on January 3rd, without a coat or jacket. Coats and jackets are not part of the wardrobe on our island and therefore not sold. My mom had a friend make a burgundy corduroy pants suit for my travel to London. Corduroy was probably the thickest fabric sold on our island at that time. I even had to wear panty hose under the pants! That in no way shielded me from what I had to face—it was a brilliant attempt though. Their winter's snow, ice, and very cold weather boldly welcomed me. What a sharp and distinct contrast to the island weather that I was used to! I knew that I had to buy a winter coat as soon as possible. Not long after that, I found out that a summer coat would be required to be part of my wardrobe. We know that type as a trench coat.

The buildings seemed to be tall, dreary, grey, and old with absolutely no colors. The black cabs, red double decker buses and mostly Caucasian faces seemed to hurry by in a blur exploding all at once. Everyone seemed to be in a big hurry, rushing to get somewhere—whew! Needless to say, it was a shocking revelation as I desperately tried to grapple with my new and oh so different environment!

The school was on the outskirts of London approximately one hour by train. I had to figure out the train system, buy the correct ticket and ensure that I was on the appropriate platform. Trying to concentrate while the elements of the weather was beating me up was most frightening and not a bit of fun. This I can tell you was no easy task particularly because it was a very cold day, and I was in dire need of a coat. When I arrived at the school, I found out that there was a hospital also located on the campus grounds. To my delight, I found out very quickly that I had landed in the midst of an International group of people. We all came there, trapped in our own unique ways of thinking and relating to people who looked, and thought like us. Well, those ideas were about to change very quickly, and all for the betterment of my growth and maturity.

Realizing that each person had their own tendencies, personality traits, and cultures, allowed us to grow closer to each other. We learned to appreciate and accept each other in many ways. We found community, encouragement, connection and shared our cultural differences by participating in each other's religious and many social events. Sometimes, we tend to believe that the world we come from is the only way that we should see things. I allowed myself to embrace many opportunities to share food, dance, prayer meetings etc. with people who were outside of my little world.

As I discovered their worlds of different doctrines, food, and clothing, it felt like I was owning many fine and precious pieces of jewelry. I was very shy and did not socialize with a lot of people but all the same I embraced the substance of my new environment.

As I recall my nursing school experiences, I am very appreciative of our professors. They were firm, but personable while they skillfully guided us through our rigid lectures. One of them had a mantra where he would say: "Do it, die, or run away." His "no excuses" way required us to be always present for classes as well as exams. Another professor told us: "There's a piece of madness in all of you." Meaning that there is something inside all of us that we care about very deeply. I was still in my late teens, so I certainly did not understand how profoundly deep those statements were and how they absolutely pertained to me. Since then, I HAVE found what my piece of madness is—yes, mine is Carnival!

They did not slack up with us and for that I am forever grateful. Our classes were small, and very conducive to maximizing our learning experiences. You felt that the professors cared and we all desperately wanted to succeed, make our families proud, and move on with our lives.

Our campus housed the school, the hospital, an adolescent unit, an occupational therapy center, a "mom and pop" store, a cafeteria, our dorms, and a social club. We attended classes for a month or two, then were assigned to various specialty floors of the hospital to receive the practical experience pertaining to the theory of our subjects. The head nurse was responsible for ensuring that we completed every element assigned by our syllabus. This experience mirrored the theory we had just received in the classroom.

About once a month, the professors visited the head nurse (not us) on our assigned floors. They checked on our progress thus ensuring that our requirements were being satisfied. We were always taught to be strong leaders and were constantly advised and supported by our professors and other management personnel. Obviously, we all had our own platforms and educational ambitions, but we were always engaged in the upward mobility of each other. We came there with a common goal—to strengthen our knowledge, become more mature and succeed in our individual field of studies.

During my undergrad studies in Sussex, part of my syllabus required that I intern (six months) at a general hospital (commonly referred to as a secondment). Here I was able to get a lot of practical experience that I desperately needed. I would be more versed when faced with situations such as changing dressings, administering intravenous fluids, etc. Hands-on time versus only theoretical knowledge eradicates intimidation. At some stage in my internship at this general hospital, I decided I needed to study for another degree—general nursing (medical, surgical, pediatrics etc). This would make me more marketable for future jobs and, more importantly, I really liked it.

•

OOPS

One year, they were having a variety concert at our campus and to this day, I still do not remember why I decided to act the role of the male dance partner with one of my friends. We were on the agenda to dance the "bump" dance to the song "Rock the Boat" sung by The Hues Corporation. We were diligent and consistent at practicing our parts—-and then the day of the show came! To portray my role, I wore jeans, a cream long sleeved shirt and a blue cap.

While we were waiting backstage, I happened to peep through the curtains and saw that the hall was packed. I recognized many of our friends and our professors. I immediately froze and my panic cells went into overdrive. It was in those moments that I realized what I had signed up for—what was I thinking? I told my friend that I could not and was not going out there and that she should ask someone else to take my place and perform this dance with her. Because I was so terrified, I suggested the name of a guy whom we both knew. I pleaded with her to perform the dance with him.

What an absurd thing to throw at my friend only a few minutes before our live performance. What her response was, I couldn't/wouldn't repeat mostly because I do not remember.

While we were on stage, I never once looked at the audience. It must have gone very well because we received an abundance of compliments. Needless to say, that was the first and last time that I performed in front of an audience—it's just not my lane.

COPING MECHANISMS

My college days gave me a chance to achieve my independence, find my new identity, and embrace responsibility. It also gave me a chance to learn my own limits by balancing parties, my boyfriend, and study time. It was a very safe and nurturing place where we aspired to be better people, build strong accountability skills, and gracefully accept and learn from our defeats and disappointments. They were pretty much about growing up and becoming much more mature than when we arrived.

We learned about choosing friends wisely—some of whom I still keep in touch with and hold very dear to my heart. Our bond has been long lasting and consistent, and I have nothing but forever love and respect for them. We have become a part of each other's families and are a major part of my framework. As I reflect, I have known them for over 50 years, and I look forward to sharing more years with them.

The long months of cold and damp weather affected my joints in an immense way. During those early years, I often wondered what the big idea of my life was supposed to be and felt like I needed to find some clarity for my purpose. Understanding my JRA taught me enormous gratitude, lots of patience, tolerance, appreciation, caring, being exceptionally strong, courageous, and how to develop an amazing pain threshold.

In many ways this high pain threshold was not beneficial because I grew to deny that I was in pain when I really was. On so many occasions I desperately needed medical attention to alleviate the deep pain that I felt. During these times, pain in my joints was an everyday occurrence. On those days when the pain was trying to get the best of me, and trust me, there were many of them, I tried my best to let in beauty and truth while I found a way to endure my suffering.

During one of my office visits, the physician suggested that I begin a weekly treatment plan of "gold injections." That is what they called it back then, but I believe it is another term for steroids. I gave it a lot of thought and began to learn about the long-term side effects of these injections. At this time, I was fortunate to be assigned to the Adolescent Unit where I observed our young patients endure some of the many side effects of this steroid. Some of them were experiencing muscle wasting, personality changes, extreme tiredness, difficulty sleeping, and the well-known "moon faced" appearance.

This resonated with me in a big way, and I became very afraid. Once again, my divine inspiration nudged me to decide against this form of treatment. I knew that I could not stop the arthritis. I learned to live with it by self-liberating versus spiraling down into a chain of deep and negative thoughts. I was a young woman and needed to go on living.

I had to change the relationship I had with my rheumatoid arthritis (RA) by removing the emotional aspect. I learned to focus on reclaiming my life because I wanted to be empowered by a good and sound education. I wanted to achieve strength and recovery for a better tomorrow.

To do so, I needed to develop the highest degree of consistency and discipline in my acceptance of the JRA. There was absolutely no room in my life to accommodate misery. I accepted the RA for what it was and moved my entire mindset into energizing myself with what was going to be left of me if and when the RA ever left my body. Some days, I crossed many "bridges," "rivers," and "crossroads" while I pushed through many dark places finding new ways to help me cope with everything.

Even if I failed in some areas, my destination today was so worthwhile and today I am a living wonder. I refused to allow toxic thought patterns to manifest themselves. And because I am writing my story, I have dared to wonder how my life would have turned out if I had succumbed to the gold injections so early in my life.

I am so proud to say that I have been able to take on a highly active and productive life! I never lived life thinking that because I have arthritis, I should not do this or that. Even though I was very aware of the pain, I lived as normal a life as possible without stacking up excuses.

I was not about to distract myself by entertaining negative thoughts. Besides, those very toxic thought patterns would have such an impact on my life decisions and would submerge me deeper and deeper into nothingness and thoughts of unworthiness. I had to be strong and find courage if I wanted to be successful in my career.

As a young person, it is surely an immense and almost impossible principle to achieve. I was alone and had to rise up amidst these confusing and uncertain times. I have never used pain as an excuse to stop me from enjoying the beauty and happiness that exist all around me. I left it up to the doctors to worry and grasp for answers about what was wrong with me. I honestly believed then as I do now that because my body was unhealthy and broken, I should not see everything else as broken. I knew without a doubt that I was much bigger than my pain. We are all continually asked to learn how to ask for what we need but more importantly, to practice accepting what we are given. Of course, some days that was easier said than done.

We did not have cellphones back then and making phone calls to get advice and support from Mom was way too expensive. Additionally, she had spent too many years of her life worrying and caring about my JRA. It was time for me to take over and figure it out. It was not easy, but I had to drop down underneath all the uncertainties, pain levels, anxieties, and fears to find gentle reassurance and surmountable hope.

I had to find a way to master these storms of my life all the while, knowing subconsciously that they would make some of my best life stories. Instead, I got busy living and not looking for obstacles. My character had to be stronger than my circumstances. Eventually, my struggles would lead to strength.

I recently listened to a show on TV where a well-known spiritual leader described pain like this. He said: "It's like watching huge waves as they rise, fold, and subside, all the while knowing as well as believing that beneath that unraveled surface, the ocean is as calm and smooth as a baby's skin."

I didn't then and still don't contribute to pity parties and the "oh me, oh my" traits. Even today, very few people know about my JRA and that's the way I like and want it. I never have been a doom and gloom person and have no intentions of becoming that type. The basic truth is people do not want to hear about your pain every five minutes. Every day I feel grateful for this second chance of life, so for me, one of my strong beliefs is—to live is a GIFT.

Self-Assessments

Throughout those college years, I learned how to overcome some of my personal fears and insecurities. I now have a greater sense of purpose and confidence about my image. One of those insecurities was the freckles on my nose. I bought different types of creams, collagen moisturizers, face scrubs, and others that I don't even remember, desperately trying to scrub them off—but to no avail. Even though it took me quite some time, I learned to live with them—eventually. Today I love my freckles and I am proud of them. I got them from my paternal grandma—Maria! Years later, these nose freckles were passed on to our younger son. Even though they are not in his younger daughter, they may even show up in the next generation. Who knows?

Some of the other trepidations that I had was, I thought my lips were fat, my hair too curly and my forehead too big. I didn't think that I had the coca cola figure like the other girls and found myself wishing that I looked like them. Sadly, I did not realize then, that ALL I needed was already in me and that what I am will turn out to be more than enough.

I had to learn how to love myself. One of the hardest lessons for me to learn was to have compassion for myself. Thankfully, over the years, I have matured and grown immensely in my understanding that there are many different layers to loving ourselves. Learning to dig deep to find ways to love ourselves allow us to emerge, awaken, and step boldly out of our self-created shadows. Learning to completely love US, just might keep those insecurities from sneaking back in.

As I reflect, I see that those terrible inner conflicts I faced in my early life were preparing me with valuable lessons to help me manage life as an adult. I also found that they were just a few normal teenage quirks that some of us go through. But unlike then, today I have come to realize that I am wonderfully made.

I learned from my mistakes and did not defend any of them, but I have and still do, use them as teaching tools for our wonderful sons and many of my college students.

During my college years, I had two boyfriends. My first one was from Mauritius—an island located in the Indian Ocean—and the other was from Sri Lanka, an island also located in the Indian Ocean. They were very good, ambitious, handsome, and intelligent guys. Like all of us, they embraced the opportunity of migrating abroad. A career in nursing was the means to an end.

They desired to attain a higher level of education to advance them to a more profitable profession. In addition to their nursing degree, they both chose to dual enroll at the University of London to study computer science and political science degrees. Around that time, this type of education was available through correspondence course. Today I think that it would equate to online courses. The major difference was, their course materials depended solely on the mail.

These intimate relationships allowed me to be always mindful, and responsive to my desires to become uniquely equipped and independent. They inspired me but I needed them to go, for me to obey the call and go on my own quest. I had to find the courage to be authentic and not be what others had branded me to be. Without a doubt I knew that I definitely was not fool enough to be in anyone's shadow and that I was not meant to be a possession.

At that time, I did not love some aspects of my life and it was solely my responsibility to change it. My happiness, total contentment and peace of mind was not dependent on anyone but myself and I chose not to be a part of their lifestyles by moving on. I saw their method of love very clearly and chose not to be a part of their cycle anymore. I have no doubt that they both loved me with all that they had, but I needed more than their type of love. They did not love me the way I wanted and needed to be loved. I "loved" them but all the while I kept them at a safe distance.

What that level of love was at that time, I really could not tell you.

Even though I came from a humble beginning, I never felt unlovable or unworthy of love because Mom worked "overtime" on disseminating her love and caring on us. I knew without a doubt that I was very worthy of true love and I certainly did not need anyone in my life who just did not support my views. I was not about to permit these romantic relationships to overshadow what was already ordained as mine. Loving ourselves is one of the bravest things we can/will ever do. I had no doubts that those environments were not right for me and my own needs were of utmost importance.

Maybe we are supposed to love someone for just a little while?

If I allowed myself to experience the fear of moving on, then I would be stuck in the same pattern of choosing partners who were not able to give me the care that I needed and deserved. Especially when they boldly presented themselves with a mindset that fosters a way of thinking that could be demeaning. I respect you, but I know myself well enough to know that I need someone who would enhance my spirit and not drain it. They were good guys and probably would have made good husbands and fathers but with someone else—not me. Little ole me simply needed to uphold my sense of self which I derived from the way my mother raised me. There was no question that my mother loved and wanted us. Despite what some of my friends thought, I refused to even focus or back track on how leaving them would be perceived or judged.

We all have our path that is already set out and designed for us to follow in this life, so I had to make sure that the one I chose was fully illuminated and not the darker one. As I write my story, I must say that I have no hard feelings, anger, or wishful thinking towards them and it is my sincere hope that they have both been successful in their careers, relationships and have been able to enjoy happy, successful lives.

Leaving them was quite easy. These experiences were good teachable moments as they related to the confines of my current environments. I

had only just conquered a minute portion of my objectives seen and un-
seen. When I left them both, I never once looked back.

London Calling

After maybe a year or so, I applied to several grad schools and was accepted by a nursing school in North London. It was very exciting living in this happening city. The transport system was so amazing and easy to understand. I loved travelling on those world-renowned red double decker buses as well as catching the tube to get almost anywhere in London.

I took full advantage of discovering all the major attractions such as Trafalgar Square, various castles, the many flea markets, and Madame Tussauds wax museum. The majestic Buckingham Palace with its changing of the guard protocol was awesome, thrilling, and breathtaking. The Tower of London with its magnificent history is a must see and is an extremely popular tourist destination.

Because I had lived in the dorms during my undergrad studies, I decided that I wanted to experience living off campus. I rented an efficiency in a little town in North London called Muswell Hill. It was a decent sized room, with a king size bed, small table and chairs, a dresser, and a small kitchen area separated by a curtain. I devised a strategy that created a functional, productive, and inspiring space that took full advantage of the natural light. My kitchen had a two-burner stove connected to a coin meter located under my sink. When I needed electricity, I had to "feed" the meter with coins.

Part of my new lifestyle in this efficiency was to always have a lot of loose coins on hand just to feed that meter. One day while I was having dinner with three of my friends, I thought that I had sufficiently fed the meter that would hopefully last until we finished our meal. However, when we were just about done, the lights went off without any warning.

I lived on the second floor, but the toilet and bath were on the third. There was a tank wall unit on the wall directly over one end of the bathtub. This tank contained the water and was connected to a meter. It had a spout at the end of it that hung over one end of the bathtub. When I needed my bath, I had to take plenty of coins and matches to ignite the pilot light. I had to ensure that I fed plenty of coins into the meter to be able to get enough hot water to finish up my bath. You know the old saying: Input breeds Output. The house was not central-heated, so this bathroom experience was a different and unpleasant experience for me. I consoled myself by the fact that this was just a temporary stop in my journey. There is no way that I could live like that forever.

My training here was intense, varied, and interesting. It was rigid and fast paced but I was able to keep up with my assignments. It became quite clear that I had to put in the work to succeed. At one point in my coursework, I needed to choose one of our professors to be my mentor. I chose our oldest who was probably in her seventies and walked with a cane. I began my sessions with her with much trepidation. I was happy to discover that she was deeply passionate about her teaching. She helped to mold and encourage me during challenging assignments. She was strict but so truly knowledgeable and experienced that I really looked forward to her classes. She showed that she cared about my well-being.

In our discussions, her intelligence and advice were sincere and solid. She was cute, infectious, and very insightful. I felt as though she really wanted me to succeed which in turn, brought out the best in me.

I leaned on her in every way that I could by adjusting a few of my old methods of studying. She was so much easier to comprehend throughout our one-on-one stints as opposed to her classroom time with us. This shift helped me accomplish my ultimate goal. Once again, my syllabus required that I complete an internship. When I received my assignment, I was allocated to shadow a doctor who was raised in the Czech Republic. The whole time that he spent with his patients, along with his bedside mannerisms, epitomized humanity in the most exemplary ways.

He devoted much of his time doing risk assessments and educating his patients about methods of prevention. Those everyday observations helped me cultivate my next step in the medical field. Before I could bat an eye, my life was about to take off in a whole new direction because I saw myself maturing to yet another level. Due to the many years required, intensity of the program, long hours, working weekends and holidays as well as being on call—that was not the life I wanted.

I decided that I did not want to waste my time becoming a doctor because my heart was not really in it. Instead, I chose to become a physician's assistant (PA). I chose it because the program did not require as many years of training compared to a doctor. This program was not common back then, but I was all about bettering myself. I began the process of applying to several schools in the USA and Canada.

In those days, before we earned our RN title, we had to take our final exams. This consisted of two parts, one practical and one theory and we had to pass them both. Six weeks later, the results came in the mail and always on Saturday! The agony of waiting that long is really indescribable. When the letter arrived, if you passed, the first words that you read was: "I have the pleasure." It was all you needed to know to start a celebration. Attaining my RN degrees was a remarkable accomplishment.

After a few months, I was thrilled, thankful and super excited when I was accepted to join the PA training program at a University in Toronto but there was a two-year wait before I could start the program. This program was fairly new at that time, and in great demand. I decided that I needed to go to the USA to work during those two years and then journey on to Toronto to begin the PA program.

REFLECTIONS

Once again, I called upon my instincts and paid full attention to this deep yearning to not stay in England any longer. This country definitely was not for me. No one or any particular circumstance had occurred to influence my decision to leave. I overcame resistance and left no room for negative patterns and made the move to pursue my calling. I knew without a doubt that my current lifestyle was not my destiny. I did not feel it in my guts, that I was experiencing the fullness of joy and believed that I needed to be in the flow and follow my divine guidance! This pursuit of seeking my real connection was the beginning of yet another part of my wonderful journey. It set me free to discover the true meaning of my success by realizing who I am really meant to be.

I believe wholeheartedly that we should give up what no longer works and find new ways of being. By doing so, we could keep close to the things and people who really matter. And so, I honored that "deep down inside" calling, knowing, and never doubting, that I was special. I felt like I needed to be treated like I was valuable and knew that I had to leave London. After much thought, research, and good planning, I somehow found the determination, profound spirit, and courage to step right on out. There was definitely somewhere else out there where I needed to be—I did not know where it was. All I knew was, I had to go and find it by taking a leap into the unknown.

I must mention that during those college years, I tried to edge God out of my life by not attending church or even praying. I felt like I was all churched out and that I could no longer identify and gain substance from the organized religion as I knew it. The church helped to build a part of my character, but the rigid organization of it left me with a yearning for a much deeper sense of conviction. But I came to realize that God is much bigger than I could imagine and that he was not yet finished with me.

Many years later, I was able to find that deeper meaning that I so needed.

At that point, my life was all about dating, studying and not too much social activities. I was so focused on my assignments that I don't remember going to many parties. I did not have a very solid plan for my life and on the day of my twenty-fifth birthday, it was as though I had reached the pinnacle of my pain threshold. I spent the day alone in my efficiency. Sometimes, I laid across my bed enveloped in immense pain from my looming/lurking arthritis. Pain was a daily event in whichever joint it chose.

Since my painful joints once again showed up and reminded me that this ailment would never leave me, I felt apathetic about celebrating this milestone. Somehow, I managed the pains by basically exhausting the phrase: "grin and bear it." I spent my twenty-fifth birthday alone.

I had experienced nursing geriatric patients who were crippled up with painful arthritis. I saw how frustrated they were because they had lost their independence and overall ability to embrace any level of a good quality of life. I was able to visualize how my life could be when I became older and for sure, it was not anything that I wished for. I could not bear the thought of a husband being burdened with my daily care during the promised aging process. I knew for sure that I would not want to be a burden to anyone so on my twenty-fifth birthday, I decided that I was never getting married and was definitely not about to have children out of wedlock.

During those years, I had fallen down the stairs many times when my knees buckled because I lived on the second floor of my dorm and my efficiency. When I used the stairs, I had to train myself to always hold on to the railings. When I needed to get to my room, I sometimes paused and mentally ran through my mind the easiest method to use in my attempt to conquer the stairs.

In no way did I regret my British experience. It allowed me to grow, and I slowly and wonderfully BECAME. I have cherished my many levels because it was the unquestionable path to my current and very rewarding destination. I was doing well there but my insides told me that I was not going to blossom the way I should. I felt that strong, passionate longing for something more. I felt out of line in my current lifestyle as though I was not in that place of belonging. I knew that now was the time to move on by paying attention to that yearning in the bottom of my soul.

While I lived in London, one of my cousins also lived there. She was a nurse and we kept in touch frequently. Occasionally I spent the weekend at her home enjoying my time with her beautiful daughter. I never went back to Trinidad until after I got my first degree—I wanted to feel a sense of full accomplishment. I honestly did not want to tell anyone that I was just a student. It would feel better to say that I am a registered nurse.

During those years, Europe was mine—it was my playground. My friend and I spent many weeks hopping from one country to the next. We caught the hovercraft over to Dover and hopped on a Greyhound bus to explore many different countries.

Roaming Through Europe

Amsterdam—This city stood out with its large unique canal system. Because they were so bicycle friendly, many of the residents and tourists biked. I was not used to this sight and found it most fascinating. I was intrigued by the methods they used to hoist furniture through a large window on the second floor. The staircase inside was way too narrow to maneuver large pieces like china cabinets, armoires, etc.

Their Tulip Festival would cause your eyes to just be transformed by their utmost beauty and it is a must see. Just watching a woman hang up her laundry on a clothesline that was at the edge of the street dressed in her traditional Dutch costume filled me with pride for her—she was even wearing her clogs (wooden shoes). The historic village settings that invite visitors to wander around farms, log cabins, thatched cottages, mills, old schoolhouses, and shops conveyed how their simplicity of life could be enough.

We visited a small town called Volendam, where the focus is on rural life. We watched the locals dressed in traditional clothing and their craftspeople hard at work as they blissfully demonstrated their methods of designing pottery and glass blowing. They were so engaged and authentic in their routines as they pridefully and happily showed off their dances with live folk music. They allowed us to dress in their clothing and happily took our pictures, some of which I still have. We attended a workshop to observe their cheesemaking process. They had at least thirty varieties of cheese shaped in the form of giant yellow wheels.

We witnessed the production process and the methods they used to skillfully carve and paint the intricate details of their clogs. While we sipped on mugs of hot mint tea, we watched a windmill turn and listened to the distinct sounds of clogs on the brick roads. I could still smell the wood fires as we savored bites of their aged cheese. Since I have never been a cheese connoisseur, my tastebuds got quite confused. Some of my favorite souvenirs were those that I watched being woven or carved.

In earlier times, their traditional but picturesque windmills helped the Dutch fight water shortages. Today they are a sight to behold. I was able to visit one of their windmills to get a better understanding of how the intricate movements worked. The working parts were made of wood, not metal, like you would expect. I understand that today, some of the windmills have been converted to actual homes!

Belgium—In their small city called Antwerp, I was drawn to their unique and beautiful Flemish architecture that was so distinct from other cities I had visited. Shopping here in this diamond trade city was a huge temptation, one that was tough to resist, and I am guilty of giving in.

Germany—I enjoyed visiting one of their charming castles, called Neuschwanstein. It occupies a hill that overlooks a small village and from the distance, it lends a striking and majestic pose. I was fascinated by the ornate designs of its chandeliers, sculptures and the number of towers. We sipped on wine from some of the wineries along the river Rhine and visited many other attractions. Their vineyards seemed to go on forever and were an exhilarating experience for my youthful eyes.

I learned how they needed to upkeep and manage the soil composition, which was unique to their particular region. They had to continuously pay attention to pest-resistant methods that ultimately led to bountiful harvests and more bottles of wine.

The Balearic Isles—Visiting here was always an exceptional treat. It is just so easy to hop from Ibiza, take advantage of nearby Mallorca and end up in Minorca. Although we were not used to it, we fully enjoyed and took full advantage of the siestas in these Spanish-influenced countries when all shops, bars and restaurants shut down and reopened after 6 pm for dinner. Sometimes I open my photo albums and rummage through those breathtaking old photos. They reflect my experiences that all the while were silently shaping my life from the inside out. I have often wondered how those countries would appear to me now that I would be seeing them through different "eyes."

Unfortunately, it has been so many years in the past, I really do not remember all the countries that I visited while I lived in England. These are only a few of them.

MY RESOLVE

My life in England felt like there was more out there, something was missing. It was like I was sitting on a beach watching all the way to the end where the water met the sky and wondering what else was out there. I could not articulate what it was, I believed that my life needed more development, mindfulness, and fulfillment and that I had to maximize who I was. I believe that there is a certain volume to life and mine was on low to moderate. For some unexplainable reason, I was restless and knew that this divine force was pulling me in another direction and that I had to align myself with it.

One thing I do know, I was not afraid to find my path and for some unexplainable reason, I found myself deeply rooted in courage, determination, confidence, strength, and hopefulness. I made the conscious decision to leave England. It had served the objective that I needed, and I used that to take me to the next level of my life's purpose.

During those years, I had attained many years of getting a superb education and I felt eternally grateful. I had also had ample opportunities to mature into a decent and marvelous adult and found so many wonderful opportunities that guided me into a very responsible individual. This was not my lane or place to stay in this life! I was so caught up in travelling through Europe and following an academic path but was I really happy? My answer was a strong no. I decided to make the move to America to experience life from a different perspective—it was a mysterious intuition, that I could not even formulate.

I had this compelling gut feeling and without reservations acted on my belief that I needed to leave and head to the US before heading to Toronto to begin my PA training. I knew my dreams were worth pursuing because I deserved them. I believed that I was never going to sit in this incomplete lifestyle and that I was not going to settle for less. Today, because of those strong instincts, I have this peace of mind inside me that tells me every day that I am exactly where I am supposed to be.

I suppose it could have been a successful and beautiful life there, but it was somebody else's dream, not mine! I knew that I did not want to be married to either of them, it was not right for me. This life that I was living with my partners was not my destiny. It was not my path. I was searching for my true self and was not about to lose my identity by becoming someone else. I knew for certain that I had no desire to live there. I needed to be the star of my life. I refused to conform to the desires and advice of others even if it meant going against the wishes of my friends and even my mother's. When I wrote to my mom to let her know that I was leaving the UK for the US, her simple but worrisome response was this: "When you get to the land of your dreams, don't forget where you came from." Hmmmm.

Stepping Out

Around May 1979, I applied to several hospitals in the US. I attended interviews by various directors at a hotel in London and received three offers on the spot. I was accepted at hospitals in Florida, Texas, and Virginia. They took care of all the legwork regarding visas and other legal documents. We did not have internet or cellphones in those days; telegrams were the vehicle they used to communicate with me and they worked quite well.

Even though I hated the cold climate and understood that it wasn't the ideal type of weather to help my arthritis, I once again allowed my divine guidance to lead me by choosing Virginia. I could have chosen Florida because my friend who trained with me in England (the same one with whom I did the "Bump" dance), had just moved to South Florida to work in the nursing field as an RN.

In England we always used the bus and Underground train system, but I knew that would not suffice in the town where I was heading in the US. During this transitional process, I worked as a staff nurse for a nursing agency on my days off and holidays to save money to buy a car in the USA. Sometimes I was assigned to nursing homes in suburban areas. These were exceptionally large, centuries-old homes converted to accommodate patients. Working night duty there would occasionally be a little scary.

The floorboards creaked, the long hallways were dimly lit, and the doors squeaked when you entered the rooms. Because I had a very clear objective, these oddities never became an issue. Instead, it propelled me to push on with my plans. I also worked at an infectious diseases hospital, nursing patients with diseases such as smallpox, tuberculosis, and green monkey disease. We had to suit up in a long sleeved white "jumpsuit," rubber boots, and a glass mask. To get to the patients, we had to put our hands through the two holes of the tent like what we see in TV shows.

I quickly got interested in this specialty. Once again, to make myself more marketable I was able to register for an accelerated course to be certified in nursing infectious diseases patients. It was super intense and moved at a very fast pace. Projects and research had to be completed and submitted in next to no time. Before you know it, I was holding my certification in my hands. For some odd reason, I wanted to experience how it felt to work at a retail store. One year, I used my two weeks of vacation and worked at a department store. I caught a glimpse of that line of work while working as a cashier and quite enjoyed it. Soon after, I was overjoyed when I received the telegram telling me that my US work visa was approved and that I needed to go to the American Embassy to pick up my travel documents. I booked my flight to the USA the same day.

Hello America

September 1979—I packed one suitcase, left everything else in my flat and left England as soon as I could to start my new job. The day that I landed at Dulles International Airport in Virginia and stepped outside the airport, I experienced moments of grandeur. I felt like I was so incredibly special, distinguished, inspired, and alive.

Two of the things I struggled with in my new environment was writing my birthdate and figuring out my race. Up until now, I was accustomed to the day/month/year format. I needed to conform to writing it in the month/day/year layout. One day, we drove past a 7-Eleven store and my birthdate issue was solved! Also, up until now, I was never once asked my race. When I filled out the form to apply for my driver's license, because of my ethnic mix, none of the boxes indicated truly described me. I left the race box empty. When the guy, who was Caucasian, observed that I had not filled in the race box, he asked me what race I was. I said: "I don't know."

To my surprise, when I got my driver's License, it had "Caucasian" in the race box!!!! Imagine that...... Driving was definitely a must because I lived in the suburbs of one state and worked in another. During my first driving lesson, the instructor had to grab the wheel when I attempted to make a left turn on the wrong side of the street. He told me that he anticipated that I would do that because he knew that I had just arrived from the UK. Folks learning to drive was no easy feat to accomplish. The roads were much wider and remembering which side I needed to be on was not only difficult but dangerous. Driving was confusing for a while, but I gave it my all. I needed to be always very alert and attentive for my own safety as well as others.

Because I had saved up the earnings from my part time jobs in England, I was able to purchase my car within the first two months of arrival.

The same day that I got my driver's license, I went to a car dealership to purchase my car. While the car salesman was trying to determine my budget and what specs I required in a car, he asked me: "With or without air? And stick or no stick?" I thought they were the dumbest questions ever. What on earth could he mean? Well, this was just another major step in my understanding of this "new world" that I had dared to step into.

Once I got all of my officially required paperwork completed, one of the first things I did was register to take the State Board exams. This is mandatory if you have a nursing degree from a foreign country and want to work in the US as a registered nurse. The next exam was scheduled for January and I had just missed the deadline for registering. I was also told that I needed to learn calculus because it was not a part of my math credits and was a requirement. I quickly went to the local community college, enrolled, and completed that prerequisite. I was then deemed eligible to register for the July exams that would last two full eight-hour days!

In the meantime, I had to work as a nurse's aide until I could take the exam and get my RN license. Once again, this did not bother me because I had a clear objective. This was just a passage to something greater. However, I must say that sometimes I did wish that I could be the RN in charge.

First Impressions

In October 1979, one month after I arrived in the US, I met Arthur Brown. Two months later he proposed and six months after, we were married. Nine months later, our first son, Arthur Jr., arrived and after two years, we welcomed our second son, Richie. One may ask, why did I get married so fast? Well, here is the sequence of events that led up to those exciting happenings.

Arthur's eldest brother, his wife and I worked at the same hospital, in different areas and on different floors. After we met, we very quickly became friends. Every time I spoke with his brother, he talked with such pride about their family's values, ethics, etc. He continuously told me that his brother Arthur was single and looking for someone who had strong principles and values. He told me how his mother and father always seemed to move in one accord. If she needed to go to the store or anywhere else, he left whatever he was doing, put his hat and coat on and happily took her.

It enchanted and fascinated me that people lived this way and it all resonated with me as a life that I would want. The amazing thing about this whole occurrence is, his brother's wife and I had countless conversations and at no time did she ever mention anything about hooking us up. BUT she was constantly calling Art to talk about and describe me to him! This blessed husband and wife never realized that they were both calling Arthur about me. They just did not discuss the idea of arranging our meeting. One day his brother was able to overhear his wife while she spoke with Art on the phone. She was scolding him because he had not yet called me.

Only then he realized that her conversation with Art was all about me! So, my dear Arthur thought there were two girls! One from his brother and one from his sister-in-law. Surprise…

About a month after listening to his brother's incessant talk about Art,

I agreed to meet him—just to get it over and done with. One Friday night he came to meet me after my 3–11 pm shift. Because this was just a temporary stop in my journey, I was not looking to start any lasting relationships, but I obliged. My job was in Virginia, but I lived in Maryland. One of the first things I told him was that I could not stay long because I had to drive from Virginia, through Washington, DC, to get to where I lived in Maryland.

We drove around for one hour and conversations were amazing and very respectful and meaningful. I told him that I would be looking to move from Maryland to Virginia to be closer to my job. Without any hesitation, he told me that I could move into the third bedroom of his house and pay him one hundred and fifty dollars a month! He owned a beautiful gold metallic, two-seater, 280Z sports car and was a member of the 280Z club. He told me that in two weeks, members of the club were all driving to visit Florida and if I went with him, he would not go with them! Whew! Two substantial offers in one hour—impressive. He also paused very briefly to show me his house.

I think that I did look at it, but I can honestly say that by this time, I was in such a daze that the fact that he owned a home just did not register any meaningful thoughts. That night, I did not find him physically attractive. We were sitting abreast of each other in the car, it was after midnight, and I really could not see his features very well. But I could tell that he had an aura of gentleness, goodness, charm, caring and kindness. In his presence, I immediately felt sweet morals and virtues and that he was embracing me and my different culture.

Being attracted to him was the furthest thing from my thoughts. What mattered to me was, I began to have that sense of belonging that I desperately needed. Of course, I find him extremely attractive now—he is my Boo! After an hour, he took me back to my car, kissed me on the forehead and gave me his number. I sat in my car unable to even think of starting it. My entire persona was all consumed with the past hour that I had just spent with him. It was as if I could feel his soul totally reaching out to me, making me feel like I really and truly mattered. I found myself magically enveloped in warmth and positive energy and I got the sense that something within me had already transformed. I was impressed.

These feelings I had never experienced before. It felt warm, safe, wonderful and different! It was as if I could see into his soul. This was truly magical, and I felt myself drawn into it as I began to connect with his spirit. That first night, something shifted in me and felt so familiar as though it was always there. Some may think it was an out of body experience that I had—call it what you will. I was completely unaware that the world even existed or that he was in his car waiting for me to leave. It was not till he knocked on my window to ask if I was alright that I found my senses.

I couldn't tell you how long an interval that was, but I knew then and there that my deepest innermost being had been touched and that my life would never be the same. And just in case you are wondering, he never touched me! It is almost as if we became intimate without having any of the physicality of it.

By the time I started my car I knew that I had to have him. I felt that I was really blessed to have my new car, this job and my nursing degrees. But this was the something else that I needed to take me to a deeper and enriched level. During this time of my life, I was not at all looking for any type of lasting love relationships other than my studies. But he had this cool, delicate energy and our chemistry was undeniable.

The next morning—Saturday—I knew that I wanted to see him but the very thought of calling a guy whom I had just met, petrified me. But a force greater than me was pushing me to do so. Since he did not have my phone number, the inevitable had to happen…. It wasn't until 4 pm that I summoned up every ounce of courage and tried to sound as casual and calm as I possibly could.

I called him with the lamest reason ever—"I forgot what you look like!" Really, Pam??? I was super delighted when he asked me to double date that night with one of his co-workers. Chemistry was overflowing as we both talked, laughed, and danced with extreme ease. There was something so natural, mystical, and so wonderful that made our souls just sing together—nothing I had ever experienced before.

Much later that night, Art asked the couple how long they thought we had known each other. Their response was two years. I believe wholeheartedly that the stage was set for my magical carpet ride! The next day—Sunday—he took me for a drive to the countryside where he grew up and I have to say that it was a day of true harmony. The vibes were nice! He was easy to be with and I knew that I wanted to be with him forever. As we drove about the beautiful countryside freely conversing, I could feel my thought process change moment by moment.

From the second that I met him and for the rest of that day, I felt transformed and even more confident. I started to realize that this was more than just a "by the way" meeting and this reality would soon start me on my new path to life. Art was very motivational, truthful, and very inspirational when he told me stories about how he was raised living on a farm. It was simplistic, difficult, and demanding. It was a delightful and very loving lifestyle with his parents and several siblings who clung to and loved each other enormously.

He is the ninth child and has four sisters who were born after him. As it was customary, the older siblings moved away to the city for work and subsequently formed their own lives there. This left him to help take care of his sisters by providing lunch, and other daily needs while his parents worked tirelessly on the farm. His gentleness for his sisters and utter love for his mother provided one of the most important prerequisites for the whole woman that I have become today. To put it simply, he gives me layers of purpose.

Yes, I had just found my husband. Everything about him felt familiar like a gentle summer breeze as though we had always been together. As we began to know more about each other, we both found so many similarities in how we were raised. Me in the islands and he in the big USA and yet we had that common thread! It's a small world, isn't it? About two weeks later, his neighbor told me that the morning after we first met, Art told him: "that he had met a girl last night and that if things worked out, he would marry her!" Thankfully, we both felt that magical element that we were searching for. After being with him for just one weekend, I went to work on Monday and headed to my supervisor's office to ask for a week off because I wanted to go to Florida with him.

Folks, this is one month after I arrived in the USA and began working and now I am asking for time off.... some nerve! When I told my girlfriend that I was going to Florida with him in two weeks, she became concerned and gave me thirty dollars to catch the bus back home—just in case (where I come from, we call it vex money). I must say that I did not share her grave concerns. I just knew that I needed to take this opportunity to know this man who had just won my heart. Our trip to Florida was about exploring our innermost feelings, thoughts, and expectations of our relationship. We spent a fantastic week with some very dear friends of his and I deeply fell in love with Florida and Art! He was easy to be with and I liked him much more than I expected.

By the time we got back home to Virginia things had moved in a very positive and committed vein. It was obvious that I came alive and believed wholeheartedly that we were moving in the same sound direction. Because I felt, without any doubt, so very loved and chosen, I moved in with him. Art simply radiates a wave of goodness, humility, and kindness as he was groomed to be by his loving family. We communicated so easily and exchanged ideas as we continued to share some of our life's experiences. We found that our basic good manners, quality foundations and lifestyles were so similar.

He had this uncommon ability to completely put me at ease and he quickly created a simple and safe space which was filled with an abundance of hopefulness and love. I always came away in great spirits and with the utmost impression that I had just met an exceptional man who had a profound and deep-rooted sense of serenity, gentleness, and respect. It was everything and more that I needed. I did not realize that I was so very much in need of this type of protection and love that he was offering. He allowed me to be who I needed to be in our world.

This truth resounded with my soul like I had never ever seen and experienced before. These basic qualities were some of what I was very much looking for but did not know how to articulate it. Without having any second thoughts, I was very willing to rewrite my priorities and plans that I had about moving on to Toronto. Sometimes in life we must go through several obstacles to get to our one true love but when we find it, life is so rewarding. I cannot be more authentically myself as I am right now, and my happiness is a generous side effect.

His Proposal

Two months after we met, we were at the dining room table having some butter pecan ice cream and he said: "What would you say if I asked you to marry me?" His proposal was actually in the form of a question and definitely a non-traditional one. But that did not bother me. I did ask him if he knew what he was saying and he said yes—I had to have him.

After his proposal, I called Mom to tell her that I was engaged. She listened carefully to my excitement and when I asked her what she thought, she replied: "Well you already told him yes, so why are you asking for my opinion?" Yes, my mother's love simply has no boundaries. Although I had not lived with her for about nine years, and I was twenty-nine, her real concern was the fact that I had just arrived in the US and talking about marriage with someone I had just met. This was only the second time that she was hearing about Art and she knew for many years, that I had sworn to never get married, so she had fathomless questions. Can you blame her?

But I knew without a doubt that my decision to marry him was like a joyful music in my head that she or no one else could hear. It was my secret and sacred melody that I clung to.

Where I come from, it is customary that when a man intends to marry a woman, he must write a letter to her family professing his love and intentions to marry. Well in no uncertain terms, my mom made this letter request known to me. Although Art was not aware of this custom, being the man that he is, he graciously obliged and complied. She later told me that she was floored by what he said in the letter. What that was, to this day I still don't know.

I believe that I was quietly searching and longing for someone to care for me wholeheartedly and that I was very open to it. We had a strong and valid spiritual connection that some may call love at first sight. I choose to say that we were spiritually, lovingly, and intellectually aligned. I believe that I was desperately searching and longing and for the exact same vibe. This ingredient would unlock the safety and love I mysteriously knew I deserved and craved, for my ultimate existence.

Our Wedding

Well folks, until now I never saw the husband, children, nor the white picket fence and definitely not a wedding. Planning our wedding in six months was a learning opportunity and an adventure. I am delighted to say that we both handled it with great joy, fulfillment, and a sense of peace while everything fell into place. My sister and my mom arrived two weeks before the wedding. When we picked them up at the airport, my mom was very tired and furious. She was bringing six large bottles of rum to make rum punch and punch a crème for our wedding guests and family members.

Traditionally, these are drinks served during island weddings and other occasions. When she arrived, she was given smaller bottles instead of the large ones that she purchased.

Now, one thing you never mess with is island people's RUM! She was fit to be tied and showed it as she fussed about the mess up. Anyway, on the way home we let my mom sit in the front seat with Art. My sister and I laughed and chatted with great excitement on the back seat all the way to our home. I was so wrapped up with listening to my sister and finally out of the corner of my eye, I did notice that Art was talking to her but what they were talking about, I did not have a clue. After we arrived at the house, my sister and I very selfishly went into the bedroom where she unpacked all the exciting things they both brought for us.

I truly was caught up in the moment and was oblivious of the fact that I had left my mom alone with Art. When I came to my senses, I saw that she was sitting at the table with a tuna fish sandwich and a cup of tea that Art had made for her. While she ate, she was very quietly looking around the rooms without saying one word. About a half hour after she finished eating, I saw her move from the dining table to the sofa. She quietly and seriously said that she wanted to talk to us and asked us both to sit next to her. I began to sweat profusely as I faced my mother who is very, very direct and never minces her words. Her surprising and brief sentence was simply this: "I like what I see, and I give you both my blessings." Whew! Imagine that, after meeting Art for the very first time, she gave me the affirmation I needed. My mom felt HIS truth.

This told me that she too believed that we were right for each other. I followed my intuition and let this divine guidance continue to lead me and did not fear for my future but welcomed it by leaping into the unknown. In preparation for our wedding, we decided that we both wanted a pound cake. We went to the local supermarket and learned that the baker was from Cuba. Because he had been exposed to the Caribbean styles and flavors of our cakes, he easily understood what we asked for. He told us that he had five-pound cake recipes and that we should come back in a week to sample. They were all slightly different in flavor but what was consistent was the wonderful texture.

Our cake had three tiers varying in sizes small, medium, and large. On either side of these tiers, one cake was shaped like a horseshoe and the other was heart shaped. Each side cake had a "bridge" that connected it to the main tiers. The main three cakes had yellow icing, the horseshoe cake had blue, and the heart, pink icing. The horseshoe represents the guy and the heart, the woman.

In June 1980, we had a simple but beautiful and sincere wedding ceremony on our driveway that was lined with green outdoor carpet. Courtesy of my dear mother, an abundance of flowers, hanging flowering baskets and beautiful red mulch, accented the surrounding areas that nestled our driveway. It looked superb and very welcoming. At the beginning of the driveway, we had a beautiful white arch covered with springtime flowers.

That is where we stood to exchange our sacred and meaningful marriage vows. Our neighbor's driveway was lined with rows of chairs that faced our driveway and became part of "the church." It was the middle of June and the weather could not be more perfect! My mom helped me get dressed and it was a special time and a treat for both of us to have some girl talk! I had five gorgeous bridesmaids who were dressed in pastel colors of blue, green, orange, lemon, and pink and they all looked amazingly beautiful. One of them was still working in London and even though it was short notice, she showed up for me.

My sister wore blue and was my maid of honor, Art's sister wore green, two of my best friends who I met in my undergrad years in England wore peach and lemon, and a friend with whom I worked in Virginia wore pink. I got dressed on the main floor of our home and Art and his five grooms-men got dressed in the basement. Art's cousin, a Baptist minister, officiated our ceremony and stood boldly, proudly, and handsomely under the arch. His beautiful wife was very instrumental in guiding the staging of the ceremony by helping us to make our entrances at the appropriate times.

His brother, who introduced us, was my "father of the bride" and proudly walked me down the aisle. One of his groomsmen was one of Art's brothers, and the others were some close and very dear friends of his. The very handsome five-year-old son of his niece was our ring bearer and as you guessed it, just stole the hearts of everyone when he walked down the aisle. We all walked down the aisle to the song "I Pledge My Love to You" sung by Peaches & Herb. Our vows and special prayers were very distinctive, and I felt such wonderful comfort, joy, and immense hope for my future with this man whom I loved so dearly.

One element that we forgot was—the rings. When we got to that part, where the minister needed the rings, we realized no one had them and Art simply and calmly told him to keep going. We later realized that our rings were left behind on the dining room table! After the ceremony, we were greeted at the entrance to our home by his mom and my mom. They received us with warm hugs, kisses, and some very meaningful words of wisdom.

Our reception was held on our backyard patio with Art's mom and sister-in-law graciously providing the dinner menu. This is the same sister-in-law who introduced us and purchased my entire bridal outfit. She would not have it any other way and even included my underwear in the bill! Art's mother bought our wedding cake and one of his brothers volunteered to be the bartender, cheerfully accommodating every request by being his usual jovial self.

We were debt-free after our wedding thanks to the generosity and willingness of my new family—the Browns.

New Beginnings

I left the job two weeks before we got married and was not fearful to let go of my career path. I was twenty-nine and my biological clock was boldly ticking away. We planned to have children as soon as we could, and we were blessed by becoming pregnant right away! It was what we both wanted, and we received the news with true delight and gratitude.

My first three months were very rough. The nausea, vomiting, and just not feeling well persisted 24/7—I even lost eleven pounds. During that first trimester because my sense of smell became so acute—it must have been in overdrive—I took to the bed and tried to sleep for most of the day. I could smell the soap in the bathroom even though no one was using it, so we all learned to keep the door closed. I felt so miserable, sick, and unhappy because of the annoying nausea. Art honored my discomforts and left his cologne and deodorant in his car.

Mom was able to stay with us for six months but unfortunately, she had to leave before her visa expired. She was superbly helpful during my first trimester and took care of the cooking and cleaning because I was in no shape to do so. I was afraid to eat because I would vomit it. I just wanted to sleep. As far as I can recall, this first trimester was the most aggravating period of my life. Can you even imagine what it is like to feel nausea and vomiting 24/7? About two months after our wedding, she saw that I was having a really rough day because I did not want to talk to anyone including Art. When we had some alone time, my mom gently said to me: Children grow old, friends grow cold, but husbands endure if we let them.

Our Handsome Sons

In March 1981, we happily welcomed our first son, Arthur Jr. Thankfully, it was an uneventful birthing process and naturally he was the most handsome baby ever! I was blessed to be able to become a stay-at-home mom with him. We believed that it was a necessary step in our attempt to empower our children with every bit of knowledge, love, and guidance. We were striving to be present in their every moment while we tried to figure out the everyday rhythms of life.

Our sons were born in Virginia and it wasn't long before I learned that being a fulltime stay-at-home mom was not in my DNA. In the early days, I ran myself ragged all day, taking care of our baby, doing laundry, cooking, and house cleaning. Since I was a new mom and wife, I had this notion that because I was at home, everything had to be done before my husband came home.

Without realizing it, I was taught that as a wife that's what I was supposed to do. I so desperately wanted to please my husband by creating a warm, welcoming, and happy household that would be grounding for the family that we wanted. One day after my darling husband came home from a full day of work, I must have looked a hot mess. He ever so gently told me: "When the baby sleeps, you sleep." He simply took him for a drive and the soothing breezes lulled him to sleep, thus allowing me to get some much-needed rest. On other days when our son was not feeling well and did not get much sleep, he did the same thing to give me a break that I needed.

I believe that I was numbing my exhaustion by rushing around creating perfection for our new family. I so wanted to hold on to my worthiness and belonging. I soon learned that I had to start learning HOW to love him. I needed to let go of those trivial and incorrect notions of what I thought our relationship should look like.

After some time, I transformed from feelings of inadequacy to I AM ENOUGH because he loves ALL of me. There is a peaceful wisdom in the way that he interprets things, and I am blessed and able to fully absorb it. Well again I say, who knew that this type of profound understanding and compromise even existed.

About two years later, we received the glorious and blessed news that I was pregnant with our second child. I chose to keep working and this time, my first three months were a lot different. This time, I experienced nausea but no vomiting and did not lose any weight! Every day the nausea occurred after 2 pm so I was able to focus on my job for the better part of the day and eat as much as I wanted.

In July 1983, we welcomed our second son—Richard (Richie). At this time, we were blessed to have one of my beautiful sisters living with us. I worked full-time and she was a tremendous asset to our growing family. She was an outstanding cook and baker. She made the most delicious cakes and frosted them with colorful, graceful swirls that left a lasting impression on everyone who attended our children's birthday parties. She took care of Richie as though he was her own. We never had to feed, cut his hair, or bathe him. I cannot tell you how helpful she was to our family and I will always be grateful for her help. She provided a valuable support system that was much needed for our growing family.

Once again, before I met Art the husband and children were non-existent in my plans. It was a lot of work, but I loved and took pride in crafting the lives of our sons. It flowed the way it should, thus allowing me to experience immense joy and never questioning my new role. Through our daily teachings we strived to focus on their daily needs (not wants). The morals and values that they absorbed were silently teaching them that input breeds output.

I believed wholeheartedly that I was intentionally called away from the nursing profession. It had served its purpose by providing a terrific education, but I chose not to revisit it. And so, with the utmost confidence, I dived into the wife and parenting profession as it spoke to me in my own life's language.

We embraced the unexpected and have raised two outstanding and very respectable young men. I caught a glimpse of what God had secured for me by becoming the person he created and knew that I could become.

Taking It All In

Life as a married woman sometimes came with its own learning agendas. I always thought that men did what they wanted and came home when they wanted with no explanations of their whereabouts or even cared what their spouses thought. No part of my DNA would succumb to that level of disrespect. In fact, that was just one of the reasons for me deciding that I was never getting married! But that type of lifestyle certainly did not apply to Art! He was proud of my academic credentials, but it was not a driving force. He was not even interested in who I had dated nor where I had been; he wanted ME, and I was enough.

In the early days I was not sure how to deal with that level of love and caring but I received it as grace. The depth of this amazing transformation took place over a period of time. I began to see my own self in a different and better way.

At times, it was difficult for me to entirely understand all this love that was so very sincere. But I drank it in one day at a time and it became so apparent that this was what true love felt like because he gave me all of his genuine self. His complete acceptance of ME helped me to identify those areas that were on medium to low. I was able to diminish their power over me and eventually see only total beauty and integrity abound. It was an honorable view! I learned to respect what he needed from me, to get what I wanted out of our life together.

Any weaknesses, fears, or insecurities died, and strength, hopefulness, true power, and courage were born. Throughout these many years, I have had some sweet moments of self-discovery. I call those—sweet spiritually filled moments. I saw myself begin to change as life naturally unfolded in front of me. I learned that it is better to love than to be right. I learned to be completely present in my new role as a wife and mother. Art showed me a bigger life than I could ever have dreamed up for myself and I became the best of me. I became much more patient and softened. Through his immense love for me, he saw me for how I so wanted and needed to be seen.

In my life with Art, I am defined by something larger. We are calm, centered, and often quiet and still. This allows any setbacks to be dealt with very easily. Our hearts are full of grace, love and gratitude that we found each other. We have managed to focus on what truly matters and doing whatever it takes to achieve positive, honest, and lasting outcomes. This lifestyle reflects our own version of happiness. I am proud to say that I am living my best life as I look forward to living each day in his presence. I learned that I mattered and my purpose in this earthly life was ordained to be with him and to raise our family.

I began to see changes in my life as I applied his love to my morals and values and enjoyed my growth. I grew in compassion and loving capability while fully embracing my new roles. Knowing myself was enlightening.

I had no doubt that I was worthy of love and very meaningful belonging. I also needed to feel that what I say means something to him. And now I believe that I have come through this corridor of figuring out my sole purpose with flying colors in this thing we call life. As my perspective of family life evolved, I began to discover that our sons and my husband had become my sacred space. This welcoming, encouraging, and unexpected experience came just when I needed it. I've since experienced that when you find the right person, there is a peacefulness and clarity that moves towards you asking for your acceptance.

I know for sure that even today, my eyes light up when he enters the room! We are magical together. I believe and understand in the power of true love—it is transforming.

I can now give and be received without judgement. No longer do I have to wonder if I matter and if anything, that I've said meant anything to him.

He is indeed my vessel of Honor.

For me, this type of love means freedom to be me, true respect, independence and deep hope. He is passionate and honest and there is a safe haven in his love because he cherishes me. We have held on to our strong principles and created a lasting partnership. This gives us an inner calm where we can enjoy a greater appreciation for the simple things of life.

I know that Providence led me to where I was truly needed and destined to be. We found ways of focusing on the things we had, realizing that the life we were building would be completely full. I view our solid relationship as being the miracle in each other's lives. It has a clarity that includes me. I have a glorious faith in him because he chooses to be at his best even when I am not at mine. He has always made what I want and need of paramount importance. I was ready and available to accept his version of true love. I saw myself as very worthy and did not need to be fixed. I have allowed myself to step forward securely holding Art's gentle hand into endless joy.

It is real, pure, and true happiness. I have a deep faith in him because he is patient and has solid integrity. He is a kind man of utmost virtue. He possesses a strong character, tremendous self-control and most importantly, he is super gentle. He has never said anything to me that's not kind or gentle nor thinks of any desire of mine without trying to gratify it. I have been living more of an awakened life.

Because he loves me, I have everything I need.

MEETING HIS IN-LAWS

In February 1982, Art, Arthur Jr., and I travelled to Trinidad to enjoy my beloved Carnival. My family relished this opportunity to celebrate Art Jr.'s first birthday there. My mom was overjoyed. She delighted in the many opportunities she had to babysit him while we enjoyed many Carnival parties and events. My younger sister was so proud of him and almost every day she somehow found birthday parties and other children's events to take him, to basically show off her nephew.

After Carnival, we visited with my father and his family and he was able to meet Arthur for the very first time. After an hour or so, he invited Arthur to go with him for a walk through his estate. Although my darling husband grew up in the USA on a farm, he had never been in such deep woods before, but of course, he obliged. It was quite a unique experience for him meeting and being alone with his father-in-law, but he managed very well.

My father must have shown him every tree he could, naming them as they walked along. He paused to cut down some coconuts, they drank, ate the jelly, talked, and kept on walking. Of course, he was trying to figure out the kind of man who was married to his daughter. It was a great idea to have some alone time for him to accomplish this.

By the time they returned from their trek through the woods, my father was looking very relaxed and pleased. He never voiced his opinion about Art or any of his observations of the woman I had become, and I never asked. Even though I was thirty-one, never lived with him, was not under his care and lived in a different country, that fear of questioning adults was still deeply rooted in me. They brought back coconuts and other fruits for us. We had a really good time joking around while we ate and enjoyed the coconut water, jelly, and delicious fruits that tasted so much better than those that we buy in the city.

My father and his wife told us that one of my sisters was living in New York and I was happy to get her phone number. When I returned to the USA in March, one of the first things I did was call my sister. Since we did not have the opportunity to grow up together, I was really excited for us to spend some quality time to understand the type of women we had become. This opportunity would ultimately deepen our relationship and cement our bond as sisters. We invited her to our home in Virginia and YES, nine months later, she flew to Virginia and spent Christmas with us! She returned several times for birthdays and other celebrations. After we moved to Florida, she spent many Christmases with us in our home.

It was quite easy for us to build on our sisterly relationship without having awkward or angry moments. Maturity and total acceptance of things beyond our control was the key to those bonding moments and it felt particularly good. From that time until now, she has been a steady companion in our home, and we have been able to maintain our weekly and, on some occasions, daily telephone calls.

She has attended our sons' high school and college graduations, as well as the weddings of both of them. Over these many years, we have been able to maintain and enjoy an amazing sister relationship without either of us ever questioning the situations that occurred when we were little. Those events had nothing to do with us and we have no intentions of having them affect us by exhibiting any type of destructive behaviors. I am honored to say that my sister is my blood, and she is a very pleasing and valuable addition to our family.

My Amazing In-Laws

I have the utmost respect and love for each of Art's brothers, sisters, and most definitely my mother-in-law and father-in-law. Two weeks after we met, Art took me to his family home to meet his parents. His mom was in her kitchen and warmly greeted me with hugs and kisses. After a while, his younger sister was setting the dinner table and I offered to help her. She told me that I should not because I was a guest. His mom promptly responded by saying that I was "not a guest but family."

This same sister became a good friend of mine and blessed us many times by willingly babysitting when we went to parties and other social events. She also honored us by being one of the beautiful bridesmaids in our wedding party. From the first day that I met each of them I never once doubted that they accepted me. Despite my island accent, they took me in and embraced me without questioning my soca music and other aspects of my culture. I may seem boastful when I say that I have the best in-laws.

If you know the Browns you know exactly what I mean. Such acceptance and love I never expected. I have always cherished all of Art's siblings and feel deeply blessed and loved. My sisters and my mom as well as some of our close friends who were considered family, felt their unique Brown's love. When we took them to visit, they always anticipated their next visit to the Browns country home.

Even though I spoke with an accent that she had never heard, I believe that my beautiful mother-in-law loved me unconditionally. I have always been grateful for her respect, kindness, and gentleness. She was always graceful and classy in the way she moved and spoke. Whenever I speak about her, I still refer to her as my Duchess.

No Bed of Roses

I am constantly reminded that Art and his family grew up during the time when Blacks were segregated, oppressed, and made to feel inferior. Despite these dismal circumstances, they still have this amazing ability to look ahead and make the best of this life rather than sit in the negativity of that era. They have not forgotten the way the American culture tried to deny them opportunities and a decent standard of education, but I am so proud to say that they've risen above, moved on, and have all been exemplary citizens. Over the years I have learnt so much about how wrong, unfair, inhumane, and broken the whole school system was for Art and his family and that entire generation who had to endure segregation.

I believe that those environments were designed by those privileged groups who were either raised to believe that they were superior to Black people or learned that type of behavior from others. Their objectives were to humiliate and oppress them in the very worst ways, simply because they were Black. Those troubled times that they had to exist in, were just so wrong. Their daily strife to survive endless back-breaking jobs were always met with humiliation while they were constantly beaten down without any chance of having a voice. These circumstances are mind blowing to me! They learned to mask the harsh, intolerable, and painful truths of their "nonexistent" lives.

This fact is deeply perplexing to my innermost soul. Their owners tried to kill their spirits by sanctioning their lives and every thought process with the ultimate goal of dehumanizing them all. No one fully knew the private moments of their lives as they desperately tried to nurse their sacred secrets amidst the daily turmoil of such intentional minimalization. It appears as though their main agenda was to assault, insult, and rape them of ALL they possessed thus spiraling them into a world of hurt. The everyday inequality challenges bore frustration and had to be met with huge compromises by accepting their world and daily life as it was.

Sadly, the plan of their oppressors was to create in their souls an inferiority complex, thus stripping away their individuality, culture, and all methods of their coping mechanisms. They tried to eradicate all their identities by imposing their white culture in every possible way, willing them to descend into hopelessness, thus destroying any chance they had of attaining freedom from slavery.

I am so glad that we no longer live in those "plantation" days that really were glorified death camps where the owners literally worked Black people to death. They took away every inch of their dignity and humanity by brushing them aside, giving rise to hopelessness with no chance of even developing dreams and visions. This ill-fated group of people were well-intentioned and simply looking for ways to survive but were unfairly cast aside as undesirable. Just by being Black, the odds were that their destinies were already plotted long before they even arrived at those plantations. They never stood any chance of being educated or even apprenticed. They exploited them for whatever goals they had in mind and regrettably used them for their own sexual and possessive gains.

Art's beautiful and classy parents had to be extra, extra strong in their character. They had to graciously guide them through those times. They had to gracefully accept what was, and not become bitter or hateful about the huge gravity of the daily struggle for equality and human dignity. It was in no way easy to accept being harassed and called the "n" word and other derogatory names, but through it all, they were able to hold their heads high and keep their dignity.

Art holds nothing back when he tells us how they had to use the old books and broken-down buses that were handed down by the other type of schools. Those schools were sanctioned to receive new books and buses— because of their favored birthright. They were the chosen skin color and sorry to say—were entitled to do so. Those were very troubling times that were so very unfair to those who were born full-blooded Americans and yet were not treated equally, and we all know the one deplorable reason for this.

Even in the workplace, they always had to prove themselves along-side others who already had a head start by being able to attend prestigious prep and boarding schools. They also had a major advantage of having parents who were educated and were thus a dependable source of knowledge.

In sharp contrast, when some Blacks were finally given access to opportunity, they struggled with learning this new way of life on their own due to a lack of the right type of support.

I find those philosophies deeply troubling and very disgusting.

I do not understand how one could come out of that era and not be biased, angry and feel hateful towards the perpetrators who executed the system. Instead, they have this distinct richness of life, a vibrancy to something so pure and honest. Art's family is blessed with a great sense of humor and being in their presence is a delightful treat.

I am blessed to say that Art's siblings are some of the warmest people you would ever wish to know. They grew up poor in material gain but so rich and classy in their values and morals. I am so very proud to be a part of the Brown family. When you are in their presence, you would never know how oppressed they were made to feel simply because of the color of their skin.

It clearly shows that where we come from, gives us the foundation of how we love. Sometimes I think we place too much emphasis on where we come from and not enough on where we are going.

Throughout our years together, like everyone else, we have lost loved ones such as Art's parents, his dad's sister, his three brothers, my mom, my father, and his sister-in-law. This has taught us that even though some have been taken away, we must appreciate those who are still here.

My infinite joy is in our journey—it changed everything. I had to reclaim some of my lost and weak self before I could grasp the true spirit of the version of tenderness that he offered me. I knew there was something very right about this relationship and that I was no doubt on the right track. I could not say exactly where this certainty came from; all I knew is my hope and desire for a better life was fulfilled and that I am doing very well because this follow-up life is oh so profoundly beautiful and safe. I feel that I am complete, very worthy, and abundant.

Being together is my most wonderful place to be.

FEELING RESTLESS

So far, I met Art in October 1979, got married in June 1980, and had Arthur Jr in March 1981. Now it is August 1981. After three months of being at home with our first son, I began to feel mentally stagnant and the need to be otherwise challenged. I realized that I did not care for the new stay-at-home-mom life. Revealing this feeling to Art was met with his full support and understanding. I registered with a temporary job agency, who told me to call them each week to check for new openings. I never did—I was still struggling with the thoughts of leaving our baby in the hands of a stranger versus going to work to satisfy my own needs. One month later, they called with an offer which I accepted. The assignment was with a tech company. They handled medical claims for coal miners by reimbursing them for their expenses. These coal miners had developed COPD—one of the many lung diseases that affected them after working there for many years.

Art went with me for the interview dressed in his usual tennis attire and carrying Arthur Jr., who was around five months old. I was dressed in a lavender dress that he had bought me for our first wedding anniversary. The fabric of this dress had an oriental feel to it, had a V neck, no sleeves, and a short slit on the side. Since I had never worked in an office environment, I did not have any of the traditional office clothes nor the typical suit that one wears for an interview. After we arrived, we were introduced to the manager, who took us to meet his wife and son. Lucky for us, they were visiting at the same time! Now how's that for perfect timing! It was an informal atmosphere "baby" chatting for a little while as we got acquainted with each other.

The interview was to be held in his office on the second floor and after a few minutes, he asked me to follow him up the steps for the interview. After we climbed a few steps I told him that I wanted to tell him something before we went any further and that he could decide if he still wanted to do the interview. I told him that I was from Trinidad and that I would be going home for Carnival in February 1982—a mere six months later. He said: "Well let's go upstairs and see what happens!" I left the interview with a two-week start date.

That weekend after church, we were introduced to a woman who was a member of our church and provided childcare in her home. She told us that she only took children who were two years and older. But when she met our adorable son, she immediately was drawn to him and agreed to take care of him. She turned out to be the best babysitter anyone would want. She was always dependable and ensured a safe environment for both our children. I leaned on her as she skillfully guided me through the different phases of their lives such as teething and potty training.

My Intro to Corporate America

On my first day in the elevator, I smiled and said a very brief hello to a woman who seemed rather conservative and shy. This beautiful woman later turned out to be my supervisor. In time, we discovered that she was born and raised in a beautiful country close to my island, and had always wanted to experience our Trinidad Carnival. To my delight, once I told her that we would be going in February she quickly bought her ticket. We all became overly excited that she would be joining us at my family's home. This was really my first time ever experiencing Carnival, but with guidance from my sister, we all had an enjoyable and fun time together.

Since then, we have enjoyed a wonderful and stable friendship with her and her handsome and gracious husband. We have visited each other's homes multiple times and have embraced strong family ties. Our relationship has lasted over forty years.

The prerequisite of this job stipulated that all new employees attend two weeks of training. It felt awesome to be in the learning role once again. During our lunch break on the first day of class, the instructor said to me: "What are you doing in this class?" She had observed that unlike others in attendance, I seemed to understand what she taught. We spoke in some detail about my years of nursing experience, and by the end of the conversation, that turned out to be my first and last day in the class. She offered me a supervisor's position in the Quality Control Department. They needed someone who had worked in the medical field to review claims that were suspended by the system for one reason or another. I had to approve or deny those claims—my first day on the job.

Receiving an office with a telephone on my desk was surreal to me. My nursing experience in England was in no way structured that way and did not lend itself to such luxuries. Once again, my life was unfolding in yet another dimension. Six months later, I was asked to teach a medical terminology class to some of the employees. Even though I had no teaching experience, I graciously accepted this challenge. The objective of this class was to heighten their ability to recognize handwritten notes that the doctors wrote such as diagnosis, services rendered, etc.

These employees were required to achieve total accuracy to be effective at their jobs. It was imperative that they understood the "language" and abbreviations used. I delved into all aspects of the objective and boldly put together a small workbook and proudly began teaching my classes. About three months later, one of our managers came into my classroom and asked me to visit with him when I took a break. A half hour later, I went to his office and he introduced himself as the project manager. He was responsible for a new account that the company had just acquired.

I would be teaching their employees all the software packages that ran on UNIX—a relatively new operating system. He said that he was building a team of twelve computer software instructors and wanted me to be part of his team. Having heard the job title and listened to what he said, I quietly asked myself if he was really talking to me! At that time, I had little to no computer experience let alone to teach it! He asked me if I would meet him for breakfast that Saturday to explain in detail the specifics of the project. He also said that I should bring my husband and our baby too.

Arthur was honored that he was invited to the interview and gladly accepted to meet up with him. It was really the best idea to include Arthur in the dialogue since he was more familiar with how the business world functioned and of course I did not. The project manager explained in detail to the both of us what his expectations and outcomes were for this assignment. Travel would be required seventy percent of the time and the training classes would consist of either one or two weeks in different states. I would be returning home Friday nights only to leave again Sunday evenings. After taking it all in, Art turned to me and asked: "is this what you want to do?"

And so, with my very limited computer experience, I followed my instincts along with the strong and loving support from my husband. I seized this unique opportunity to become one of his computer software instructors! Because of my husband's infinite presence, he played a remarkable role by offering his support and encouragement for what was about to happen. Two years later, his strong and endless influence turned out to be one of the greatest milestones that I have achieved in my careers.

Thus, began another phase in my understanding of the substance of this man, my husband. Our sons were two and four at that time and attended a preschool close to our home. This meant that he would have to leave work early to pick up our sons by 6 pm. On snow days, if there was any traffic caused by accidents or there was an accrual of snow and ice, this task was a particularly challenging and stressful thing to accomplish. He told me that he had no concerns about providing mommy and daddy duties while I was away. He also said that if the same opportunity were offered to him, he knew that I would not deny him the chance to advance his career. I cannot even begin to describe the gravity of what this situation presented for our young family.

One day, the project manager invited me to attend a welcoming and informational meeting to address the purpose and objectives of this new project. The meeting was held in a large conference room with a long table. He was seated at one end and his boss on the other. There were twelve instructors, six on each side of the table.

He spoke about the nature of the project and outlined in great detail what the goals were. He spoke for a while about the expectations, deadlines and responsibilities required from each of us. He then moved on by asking each of us to introduce ourselves and describe the type of computer experience we had! Because I had no qualified experience whatsoever, my fight or flight response kicked into high gear. Adrenaline reigned supreme.

My first reaction was to get up and run like hell without stopping. The first three instructors (I was number four), spoke about the many years they had worked in the computer field, using such words as: DOS, COBAL, Mainframe, Lotus 123, etc. The words they spoke were to me, a foreign language. I had no idea what they meant. How could I learn this stuff if all I know is the nursing language? It quickly became clear to me that I did not belong there—I was a square peg in a round hole quietly wishing that the floor would open up and just swallow me.

When it was my turn, all I could say was: "I'm a registered nurse and I have no computer experience." Yes! As you can imagine—there was a deathly silence! After what seemed like hours, the project manager very calmly reassured me that I was a valuable part of the team and that he was looking forward to working with me. Mere words could hardly describe my state of mind throughout all of this. During our lunch break, I walked out to the foyer and leaned against the wall in deep thought, deciding that I was not going back to the room. One of the instructors who was on the other side of the table, who had not yet spoken, came over to me and offered encouraging words. He tried his best to reassure me that he would help me to understand what I was required to teach. He was spot on in his exact perception of what my thoughts were during this time.

I had to learn from the ground up, it required loads of patience, diligence, and cohesiveness. In those early days, I would sometimes ask my co-workers for help in understanding some of the topics. They would answer me but because they all had so many years of experience, their explanation was at a much higher level for me to grasp. It was not clear enough for me to understand and after the second time, I stopped asking for their help. This meant that I had to dig much deeper on my own to grasp the full meaning of this new world that spoke to me in such a different language. Developing a strong set of technical skills in just a few months presented its own multitude of challenges.

After several weeks of grooming myself for this enormous task, I found myself progressing from I don't know it to I don't know some of it, to I know most of it, to I understand it, to finally saying I can teach this! My entire professional world shifted and became alive. I had to adjust, thus leaving behind what I had known and was comfortable with in the nursing world. I had embraced the unfamiliar.

Each time that I entered the classroom, I had to own my presence and find every shred of confidence to provide the best methods of instructions to my students. Because of my ability to rise up from below zero, I was able to identify with some of the difficulties my students faced. When they didn't get it, I was able to break it down in a simplified manner where they were able to grasp the concept. Their difficulties mirrored my own experiences when I first tried to absorb it. I was more than happy to extend myself by giving them an opportunity to sit with me after class to go over the material that we had covered.

As my teaching experience grew, some students were always trying to find my classroom because word got around that they should "go to Pam's class." One day, during my evaluation, my boss thanked me for being an asset to his team. He praised me for all those "all-nighters" that I had pulled in my desire to rise to the challenge that most would have either not accepted or would have caved in along the way.

There was no pretense here. I was growing in yet another path and loving it. Having been given this opportunity to travel and teach, I fully embraced it. I treated it as though I would probably never be able to get back to these places on my own dime. Wherever I went, I took advantage of what was happening in that city. One of the things I did while I travelled for this project was to get recommendations from the locals of places to eat that were outside of the tourist areas. Most days after I dismissed my class, I always made sure that all my software programs were loaded for my next classes.

After tidying up the classroom, I headed out for some adventure. Once, I attended a fashion show held at a center that was close to my hotel. At the end of the show, we were able to buy the clothes that were modeled. One of the hotels where I stayed, owned a jazz club just across the street. All guests were admitted free so yes, you know I was there every night after work. It was at this club where I was able to enjoy performances by Wynton Marsalis—an incredibly talented jazz trumpeter.

One of my many road trip experiences occurred on the outskirts of town in Ft. Worth, Texas. I went to a small top-rated barbecue restaurant that the locals recommended. When I got to the front door, I felt like all eyes turned toward me. Moments of anxiety, adrenaline and second thoughts enveloped my entire body. Yes, you guessed it—no one looked remotely like me. Thoughts of *Do I dare go in or do I just backpedal out of the door?* began playing in my brain—*what were you thinking!* Heralding every nerve in my body, I decided I would give it a try.

Country music was playing, and it had a nice beat to it. While I ate, it was very normal for my head and feet to pulse to the beat of the music. I have never been able to hear music and not respond in some way. Even when I was in high school, I never could focus on doing my homework if the radio wasn't on. Today, yes, you guessed it!!—while I am writing this bio, I do have the radio on.

The barbecued ribs and side dishes were simply amazing, very tasty, highly recommendable, and I fully enjoyed every bite. Just as I was about to push back my chair to leave, a tall, burly, red-bearded man with bib overalls that had one strap off his shoulder, walked up to me. With his arm extended and with a very deep husky voice he said: "Wanna dance"? Folks, to say that I was a little terrified is an understatement. I suppose he was either trying his best to be hospitable or making the best of a dare—I obliged.

Now, country music is not my genre, but I have always loved dancing even though while I was growing up I did not get the opportunity to do so. When we got to the dance floor, I was very relieved that he had good rhythm and knew the steps to the dance which he told me was the "Cotton-Eyed Joe." The steps were quite easy and repetitive. In no time I was line dancing! This song rolled into another and we kept on dancing. I must say I really enjoyed it. He wasn't very talkative, just gentle, and I was relieved that he held me at arm's length. I am quite sure that all eyes were on us, but I was very oblivious to any of that. After two dances, he asked for another, but I graciously thanked him and left. Because I dared to try something new, I had a wonderful, enjoyable, and most memorable evening.

During some of my lunch breaks with the students, I learned that in Texas they take serious pride in their culture, especially with their boots. Some of my students had theirs fitted and handcrafted in boot shops. Each day, the men wore their traditional western styled plaid button-down shirts, jeans, large- buckled belts, leather boots and not to forget—their western-style cowboy hats. Most of them had a moustache or a beard and had either a brown suede vest or a black leather one.

During the two years that I travelled, there was never a time when I came home for the weekend and had to do laundry or housework. Art saw to it that I was fully energized to head back on Sunday evenings. We managed this arrangement for two years without even one hiccup—thanks to his due diligence and belief in what I wanted to accomplish on a personal level. Around this time, I received an offer from the director of the IT department to become a systems engineer. This was a rewarding program that would elevate my skills and propel me even further in the computer engineering field. I did my own research and found that it was demanding, extremely time consuming, and an intense program that would last two years. The regular 9-5 hours would be non-existent.

As I thought it through, there was one prerequisite that I could not and surely would not succumb to. I was required to sign a contract that compelled me to work for the company for two years at the end of the training. I felt deeply honored to be chosen, but in my mind and soul, I was not about to sacrifice my family any longer.

CHANGES MUST COME

One day, while I was in my hotel room, I decided that this two-year road assignment had to end. Art's dad was hospitalized with a stroke. He was unable to visit during the week. I subconsciously became aware that ambition could gradually overtake and consume me if I pursued it by advancing too fast. I believed that being at home with our family would provide a better and generous version of me. I must say this husband of mine never once complained but I made the decision that I needed to speak to my manager regarding terminating the assignment. At my request, they offered me a part-time position working with the US Customs department on Constitution Avenue in the heart of Washington, DC! Being home again every day, with my family surrounding me, served us well in so many ways.

A few years later, Art's job offered a sweet deal for employees to leave the company if they met a certain criterion. This package included two years of health care coverage, money to get educated in another career, coaching on how to write resumes, etc. It was a very fair and encouraging offer. We discussed the notion of signing up for the offer and using this great opportunity to fulfill our dream of moving to Florida. By this time, I had already cultivated an awfully close relationship and cared deeply for both my mother and father-in-law. I wanted to be part of caring for them when that time came. He felt that we should take advantage of the opportunity.

This sound advice proved to be the best idea for our family in so many ways. This package fulfilled our wish to move to Florida even though we would have to seek employment elsewhere. In October 1988, with careful financial planning and much excitement, we headed down to the west coast of Florida. We bought a house, intending to move there two months later—the beginning of January. About two weeks later, even though he had already signed up to leave the company at the end of December, Art was presented with an amazing and very lucrative job opportunity. He was offered a job with the company to work in Boca Raton on the east coast of Florida. He gladly accepted the job offer but was required to begin working there within a week or two.

Our situation became a little complicated, but we handled it with grace as we always have done. We had just purchased house number two on the west coast of Florida, we needed to sell house number one in Virginia, and we needed to buy a home in Boca—house number three. We have been eternally grateful to my younger sister, who was able to stay with our sons for a week, thus allowing me to meet Art in Boca to purchase a house there. This act of love from my sister was, and still is, valued and treasured. I just don't know how we would have been able to accomplish this task without her.

South Florida Living

Our first three days of house hunting were not fruitful. Not one of them "spoke" to us. By the end of the third day, the agent said that the next day, she would take us to the neighboring city called Delray Beach. We had never once heard of Delray but willingly went with her and found that it was the neighboring town, just about fifteen minutes away from his job. As luck would have it, the first house that we saw in Delray is the house that we still live in—32 years later.

Our sons were six and eight when we moved to Florida to enjoy the many years that have shaped our family into total fulfillment and wonder. They began school in second grade and kindergarten. It was an easy transition with the enrollment process, and they settled in quite nicely. One of the highlights of my days was watching them ride their bikes down the sidewalk to their school about a quarter mile away from our home. When they got to an area where they could no longer see me, they would both look back and wave.

The school is so close to our home that sometimes, you can hear the school's marching band practicing and the announcements on their PA system as they prepared for school dismissal. In the afternoon, I waited until I heard the voices of the children, as they walked home playing and squealing in delight. I promptly went to the front yard to watch out for our sons. Once again, when they got to that area where they could see me, we would all experience that "happy to see you" wave. Being able to be present for them during those times has been one of my lifetime trophies.

I never really knew that I had the capacity to help our sons fulfill their dreams. I quickly realized that my best attitude elevated their attitude. Because we were happily emitting positive chemistry, we were able to give them 100 percent of us. Some of my very special moments that I recall is watching how very cohesive our sons were with each other as they focused on that special magic of their friendship. It was authentic, supportive, and influenced each other while they worked on developing their own personalities. It was fascinating to watch their genuine care for each other. Many times, I captured their interactions, and I was overjoyed to observe that it seemed like they functioned as though they were one unit.

They were receptive to our lifestyle and teachings. We never tried to compromise our core values, purpose, or behavior while sharing on a daily basis, our own guiding principles. Interacting with them, is uplifting as I discovered that their intention is to enlighten and inspire me to be always mindful in their presence. We trained them not just HOW to accomplish but how to BE. We so wanted them to get to the top of the right ladder. We made an extreme effort to furnish them with all the tools we knew to help them figure out if their ladder was leaning against the right wall.

I am proud to say that they emit gentleness, goodness, patience, simplicity, pride of who they are, and humility. For me, having the best character weighs heavier than having a great career, or the highest GPA score.

One of the first things we did after our move here was to enroll our sons in the Florida Pre Paid College Program. This act proved to be one of the best decisions for our family. After five years of paying for it, their tuition plans were paid in full, thus assuring them of a college education when that time came. In essence, they grew up knowing that they would be able to go to college many years later. We are happy and proud to say that they both never had a student loan to repay.

When we moved into our home, there was a family who had two children the exact ages as our sons. They instantly became friends and spent summers in the pools at each other's homes. Throughout those many years, we never once heard anyone getting into a clash or not wanting to spend time together. On many occasions, their sweet and loving grandma who was a highly active one, took all four of them bowling, golfing, etc.

A few weeks after we arrived in Florida, it was Easter Sunday. We decided to visit a neighborhood church. When we got to the front door, the service had just started, and they were already singing the opening hymn. I quickly observed that the ethnic composition of the congregation was quite unlike us. I stood there for a few moments just frozen. My thoughts were that we should step backwards and leave. Before I could say a word to Art, this broad-shouldered, beefy looking guy with a warm and comforting smile extended his arm and escorted us to the first pew—the only empty row! Mere words could hardly describe how terrifying each step felt as I knew that all eyes were on us.

This was the beginning of our spiritual growth and that was exactly what our family unit needed. Our church family embraced us and some years later, our sons and I were baptized at different times and we became members. Over some time, Art was selected, mentored, and ordained by the pastor as a church deacon. He was involved with managing the personnel issues and several other tasks concerning our church. We joined the choir and taught Vacation Bible School as well as Sunday school and absolutely enjoyed every bit of it. Our sons were involved in various church groups such as playing hand bells during our Sunday services. They also participated in numerous activities such as building cars from pine wood wooden blocks for the car derby. It was one of the best opportunities for dads and sons to get creative by building, creating, and shaping their cars being mindful of what the restrictions and rules involved. This was one of the best family friendly competitions and it was a beautiful and encouraging thing to see our entire family moving harmoniously within our church. Being spiritually involved, gave us all a good solid community that fostered a sense of belonging.

To keep my brain active, I took a part time (10 am–2pm) data entry job and was adamant that the hours could not interfere with their school hours. I chose not to have any type of job responsibilities that would distract me by being too demanding of my time. I wanted to be fully present in our home not only when our sons left but more importantly when they returned from school. A few months later, I was offered an accounts payable position and an invitation to come on board full-time. Because I did not want to get too involved and heavily burdened with project assignments and deadlines, I compromised by increasing the hours to 9 am–3 pm.

I couldn't/wouldn't commit to any more promotions. My priority was being there and having the time to fully focus on accommodating and fostering our sons with the demands of school projects and sports. This was of paramount importance to our solid family unit, and I refused to allow anyone or anything to change our rhythm. We focused on providing them with a solid structure by offering them an unceasing flow of love, unified behaviors, and conflict-free guidance. Any advancement in my career had to wait.

I am grateful that during those years, we were able to manage financially which gave me that option of occasionally working part-time. I had walked out into a new self that was immersed in the development of my family. I was happy and didn't feel guilty about my absolute happiness. Today, it's infinitely rewarding to observe how our sons interact with their families. They are ambitious, kind, gracious, they boost our happiness and are a priceless part of our lives.

Being ever present to offer our support was always there, and I would happily embrace the idea of doing it all over again. I believe wholeheartedly that I have fulfilled my soul's purpose. We have given our sons the best moral compass and displayed the power of kindness by our words as well as our actions. Education nor money does not make you happy or successful, but love and family are two of the best things we have. Our sons knew that they were special, deeply loved and cherished which is such a huge part of the equation for raising our children.

Keeping in Touch

Many years after we left Virginia, we continued our annual visits there. We strived to keep our sons linked up with their father's family. Those were years filled with wonderful and exciting visits to their aunts, uncles, and many cousins. Our sons were raised to be proud of where they came from and I have no doubt that they know who they are. Most importantly and special were our visits with Art's mom, especially when she made her incredibly delicious dinner rolls.

Before we left for our visit to Virginia, we always visited the library, which resulted in armfuls of books that they always enjoyed reading along the way. We made sandwiches and packed different snacks and fruits. We filled up a cooler with a variety of soft drinks and loads of ice. When we made a pit stop it was only for gas and to use the bathroom. We always made the trip in two days because we wanted to spend a cozy night in a hotel only to enjoy that different aspect of life on the road together.

Because their chemistry blended so well, our journeys were always enjoyable and soothing. This factor allowed us to seize every moment of this quality time. The fact that our sons always got along made those trips stress-free. There were never any fights, arguments, or the famous phrase: Are we there yet? They always remained calm and patient thus allowing us to maneuver the highway in the best way possible.

Those trips back to Virginia have been and still are such a joy. We enjoyed the majestic mountain views, different designs of the homes, good ole country foods, rolling hills, bales of hay and the miles and miles of vineyards. We usually paused to visit the small quaint stores that have stood there since Art was growing up. Their churches are small and still have wooden benches minus large television screens and fancy, modern, and unnecessary stuff. The outsides are usually white-washed, and some seem to be hidden deep in the hills. The décor was always humbling with simple wooden unpadded benches. One very happy factor that still exists is, you can still find a Bible and song book located at the back of each pew. Stepping inside these rural churches always stirred up his childhood memories which he gladly shared with us.

This is a place where you slow down and let adventures unfold. It reflects and reminds us of the simple and happy serenity of life we enjoyed not so long ago. History shows itself when we pass rivers named the Big Indian Stream, the Jordan River, and the Rappahannock River. I smile in deep appreciation and respect when we drive past old stone walls. I tried to imagine, without any success at all, the blood, sweat, tears, and sheer disrespect for humanity that were lost while they were being built.

During those trips, I am always awe struck by the intoxicating beauty of the Virginia countryside. Some of those winding country roads lead through mountains where the road seems like it would almost touch the edge of the trees. I seem to lose track of time when I am there. Something in me finds a different rhythm as I allow myself to give in to nature and slowly but surely it takes over me while I inhale ALL of it! I know that it is always there waiting for me because it agrees with my nature. I am at home, just listening to the sounds of the cicadas, the gentle fluttering of the leaves, and the gorgeous cardinals. I am at peace watching the quiet streams and rivers flowing peacefully by in their quiet way.

In the last five years, we have been making an annual trip back to a small town called Flint Hill to be part of the homecoming celebration of the church where Art and his family grew up. Back then, the church served as a place of comfort, belonging, safety, and a great source of community where they shared ideas of coping with segregation and injustice. It's a sincere joy and delight to return each year when he gets to meet up with his precious cousins, her husband, and other family members, friends, and former classmates whom he hasn't seen in a while.

When they see us, we are always able to sense the love and happiness that emits unique genuine love. The service is always very uplifting as they celebrate each other. If you ever wanted to experience a joyful, full of praise, spiritual, and harmonious church service, this one is it! The music from their saxophone, organ, and piano causes us all to react by foot stomping, head nodding, hand clapping, and body shaking.

After the service, we get to indulge and thoroughly enjoy a great meal that is good ole country cooking at its finest. It is a refreshing and wonderful time to sit with family and friends to catch up on the latest news of their families and about their daily lives. On our way home, we enjoy taking a breather to visit Warrenton, one of the small towns where Art grew up.

Photographs

My mom Janie, in a three-hour layover at Ft Lauderdale airport after visiting Trinidad in 2010

I embraced the chance to see my mom in her layover stop at Ft Lauderdale airport in 2010

Pam and her sisters, with Mom in the center (L to R): Brigid, Pam, mom, Gloria and Jean at her home 2015

Pam's maternal grandma Agatha at her mom's home while we were visiting Trinidad 1984

Pam's maternal grandma Agatha visiting the island of Grenada around 1967

Pam's maternal great grandpa (Agatha's dad)
who was born and raised in India

Pam's cousin Mike took her to visit the remnants of her grandma's beautiful house in Coryal, Trinidad, 2015

Pam's father Riley, around 2001, right after being diagnosed with colon cancer

Pam and her father at his house in Tamana, Trinidad, after Carnival, around 2000

Pam's paternal aunt Ellen (age 93) at her home in
Tamana, Trinidad, 2017

Pam's paternal grandma Maria, who was born
and raised in Portugal

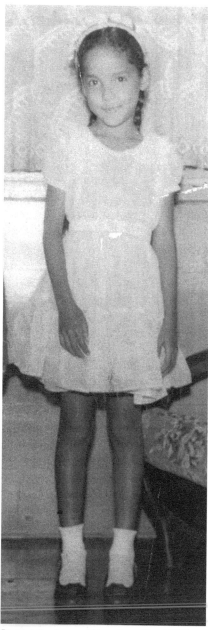

Pam at the home of her dear friend Hillis,
in Arima, Trinidad, in 1960

Pam employed at EDS as a Computer Software
Instructor in 1987

Pam relaxing at Brighton Beach, England,
around 1973

Pam attending a wedding in Haywards Heath, Sussex, England, 1974

Pam's mom and elder sister Jean enjoying our Thanksgiving holiday, 2005

Pam's sons and nephews (L to R): Richie, Dean, Arthur Jr
and Marty, Clearwater, Florida, 2019

Pam's youngest sister Gloria, (the chef for our
Christmas parties) at our home, 2019

Pam's nephew Randy (her sister Gloria's son)
at the airport, around 2012

Pam's sister Brigid and Arthur in our
kitchen at our Christmas party
around 2010

Arthur's oldest brother Carroll in 1979, who
introduced us

Pam and Arthur after their wedding vows on their driveway
in Virginia, June 1980

Arthur's parents, Mr. & Mrs. Frank and
Edna Brown

Pam's mother-in-law Mrs. Edna Brown at her
home in Virginia, around 2002

The house where Arthur and his family lived in
Crest Hill, Virginia

Our precious sons, Richie (L) and Arthur Jr,
on our back patio 2019

Pam and her daughters-in-law, Janelle (L) and Crystal,
Christmas 2016

L-R: Arthur Jr, Arthur Sr, Janelle, Pam, Crystal and Richie around 2010

Arthur Jr & Janelle's son Caulen (age 7)
with his French bulldog, 2020

Richie & Crystal's daughter Kayleigh, (age 4)
Christmas 2020

Pam's high school graduation, from
St Joseph's convent, St. Joseph Trinidad 1969

Pam and her cousin Kathleen, at Miami airport
on their way to St Kitts/Nevis, 2017

Pam and Arthur in their Carnival costumes at their B&B Woodbrook,
Trinidad, Carnival 2014

One of the many beautiful Trinidad Carnival costumes on stage in front
of the judges

Pam and Arthur in Indian attire attending a family's birthday party, 2014

Pam and Arthur dressed to attend their friend's Poojah, 2015

Arthur at my cousin Murch's home in
Louisville, Kentucky, around 2019

Arthur relaxing and taking in the
beautiful views in Siena,
Portugal, 2018

Pam taking in the unique spectacle of Bern, Switzerland, 2018

My mom's beautiful crafts and handiwork displayed at her memorial service, 2019

Pam taking a moment to relax at their home in
Alexandria, Virginia, 1981

Pam and her cousin Mike at our family friend Clinton's house in Trinidad, 2017

Our World of Sports

Our sons were always actively involved in various sports like baseball, golf and tennis. They embraced those experiences and learned to build positive relationships with other team members, principles of good sportsmanship, doing what's best for the team, trust, and discipline. I prepared a home cooked meal for our family every day. On days when there was a game or practice, I took Art's dinner to the baseball field where he joined us after work. These games usually finished late. He ended up eating his dinner seated in our car in the parking lot.

Because of their age difference, the games were sometimes held on different fields. Art and I switched off midway during the game just to be present for all their games. These were terribly busy times, dropping off, picking up and having their baseball uniforms washed and ready for the next game. Those games during the week sometimes ended after 9 at night so once we got home, showers and any unfinished homework were of utmost importance.

In his earlier years, their dad had taught himself the game of tennis by hitting against the back wall of his apartment. His self-taught techniques progressed to where he played on the B league team at his job. He was able to teach the game of tennis to both his sons on our driveway as well as our cul-de-sac. Richie took to this game of tennis like he was born and ordained to play. From second grade until he graduated from college, our weekends were all about attending tournaments in one city or another.

Throughout those years, other dads and moms questioned Richie's dad about who trained him and what methods he used to cause him to be so calm and respectful whilst on the court. Arthur Jr also learned the game of tennis, played a few of our local tournaments but chose to pursue golf. In his junior year of high school, he was selected to serve as a Senate page in Tallahassee, Florida. This is a very selective, prestigious program that provides students with an opportunity to play an active role in the daily duties of the senators by attending classes and debates with them.

HOSPITALITY

One year, we saw a sign at our tennis center inviting volunteers to host young people from different countries competing in a tournament in our city. Being a volunteer meant that there was no financial assistance, and we would be required to provide housing, meals, their laundry, etc. When we signed up, we stated that we would host four males. We thought that there would be common grounds for them to get along with our sons. Without hesitation, we signed the necessary forms and began to willingly provide all the assistance required for their stay.

For many years, we hosted these young tennis players who were seeking to make their entry into the tennis world by accruing a maximum amount of points each time they won. In the tennis world, it's referred to as "chasing points." Our USTA tennis organization offers junior tournaments for the younger players.

This allows them to compete and in time, secure a junior ranking before they become eligible to compete in professional tournaments.

Some of the many players whom we hosted came from countries such as the Bahamas, Spain, and the Czech Republic. We enjoyed whatever cultures each group brought to our home. What a joy and fulfillment it was as we all embraced them. In return, we asked them to teach us about their customs, foods, etc. The first group that we hosted were four young men from Spain.

The first morning, when I went to the dining room, I greeted them and saw that the four players were all happily sitting at the table chatting away and comfortably eating. The gallon of milk, loaf of bread, different boxes of cereal, butter, jam, gallon of juice, etc., were all on the table! They explained to us that meals were a social event that lasted an hour or more so rather than going back and forth, they simply brought all that they needed to the table. We were so happy to learn about this aspect of their culture and even incorporated this idea into our mealtimes.

They enjoyed watching basketball and at that time, one of the Spanish players was a huge fan of Shaquille O'Neal. When he watched him play, he squealed in delight: "O'Neal, O'Neal." It was a joy to listen to the laughter as I watched our guests embrace each other playing video games with our sons. Even though there was a language barrier, there was a distinct human element that we all felt. At no time did we ever wish we had never extended our hand to accommodate them in their journey. I am overjoyed to say that several years later, three of those players whom we hosted from the first group, were successful professional tennis players. They attained individual world rankings as high as number 5, number 12 and number 34.

Over those many years, we developed a very close relationship with one of them and he has been embraced as our "son." Whenever he came back to South Florida to compete in tournaments, he took the time to spend a few days in our home before moving on to another state to compete or return home to Barcelona, Spain. He is retired now and lives in Barcelona with his family, coaching up and coming players who are also looking for a ranking and their spot in the tennis world. In October 2018, we made the trip to Barcelona for our "honeymoon." We were able to visit his home where we met his beautiful wife, gorgeous children and very friendly in-laws. They all knew about the many times that he spent in our home. It was a homely and very comfortable experience. He proudly showed us around his beautiful country.

When we signed up to be a part of the hosting program, we stated our preference for having guys vs girls. It was a natural thing to do only because we had two sons and thought that there would be more common grounds. One year, we found out that the tennis center was desperate to find a host family for two young ladies from the Czech Republic and we gladly accepted these beautiful young ladies. Whenever we took them to the supermarket they were always thrilled about the large containers of our gallons of milk, OJ, etc. They gazed in disbelief when they saw the large size chocolate bars and the countless varieties of cheese and rice. Every item seemed so massive to them. They told us that in their country, they had to go to the store for their daily rations and were used to receiving only quart sizes of milk and other items. This experience was one of the reasons why one of them wished that she would be able to visit us again. For various reasons this never happened.

They wanted to prepare for us Chicken Paprika, which is one of their national dishes. To this day, this unique, delicious experience sticks with me. We bought one whole chicken. They cut off the meaty pieces and placed them in bowl number one. All scraps of meat left on the bones were scraped off and added to bowl number two. The bare bones went to bowl number three. Bowl number one was made into the very tasty, creamy tasty dish called Chicken Paprika. Bowl number two had rice, black pepper, salt, and other spices added to it and cooked down. Bowl number three was boiled and seasoned by adding carrots. It turned into a flavorful and scrumptious brothlike soup.

They told us that each of those dishes would be their meals for three days! We on the other hand would use that one package of meat, make those three dishes and have them all for one meal! Lifetime survival lessons to be learned! These valuable teachings were priceless for all of us.

I believe that we made an unintentional effort to be a good force in people's lives. As a result, we were able to inspire and teach day-to-day positivity that was useful and meaningful for their futures. We were able to form a community of people who have been and are still impacted by our examples that still is a viable part of them. Those experiences will live on far beyond our lifetime into their spouses and kids and that for us is a thrilling reward.

Our children never forgot those years of these valuable life skills and experiences. It was not all about what we did but WHY and HOW we did it. Through these basic humane examples, they were delicately building very strong characters and a significant value system.

Our Sons' College Education

Arthur Jr. and Richie completed their post-secondary education by attending our local universities, all the while living at home until they graduated. We believe that this set the tone for their adult life. We were both close at hand to offer solutions and advice if anything became an issue. We took pride in guiding our children through their educational journeys using some of our own skills and experience. It was calming to observe them while they mastered their instruments of morals and values. We observed how their skills for time management, punctuality and taking responsibility for their own actions were exploding daily.

Fortunately for us all, they both sailed right through those years and were able to graduate with their bachelor's degrees. Arthur Jr worked nonstop from the time he was in high school and throughout his college years mostly at golf courses. He built many valuable friendships with some of the residents of the golf clubs. He learned and appreciated how "their culture" worked for them. Whenever he could, he took advantage of playing golf with a few of the residents. He played golf with different groups of friends from our church and high school. He was able to beat the son of one of the high-ranking golf players in a qualifying game to be able to play in the main draw of the tournament.

He also enjoyed his dirt bike sessions with his friends on Sundays. He competed in a few local golf tournaments but unfortunately between the dirt bike sessions and golf, he messed up his back and sadly had to put an end to those sports. About six months before Arthur Jr graduated, through the assistance of a friend, he was able to begin working at one of our local financial companies. He was very motivated when they told him that if he performed well, the company might want to recruit him as a full-time employee once he graduated. Regrettably, nine months later, the company was bought out and being one of the last ones to be hired, he was laid off.

He was devastated because he really liked the career of being a bond trader. Within a couple of weeks, he began working at our local credit union. He enjoyed it but felt something was lacking.

Lucky for him, two years later, that new company was bought out by another company who were hiring. One of his co-workers put in a good word for him, he was called for an interview, and got re-hired! This field has charted a course that has grown into a lucrative career that he still masters today. Currently, he's the senior vice president for his financial company. His accomplishments are some of my proudest moments. He has emerged as a very mature, practical, and well-groomed young man, mimicking good business sense that he learned from his dad. He is the kind of son everyone dreams of, but he is MINE!

In October 2007, he and his beautiful long-time girlfriend were able to buy a beautiful home about half a mile north of us. One year later, in November 2008, he married her. In February 2013, we were all blessed by the birth of their handsome son. Some years later, even though he had a full-time job and a young family, he took online classes in his quest to obtain a master's degree. It was not easy working all day, spending time with his little son as well as his wife and still finding the time to study in between all of that. Sounds like immense self-discipline and commitment to me! Armed with sheer determination, conviction, and confidence along with the loving and wonderful support of his dear wife and son, he was able to obtain his master's degree.

❧

During his high school years, Richie's tennis skills were apparent and promising. He was selected to serve as the number one player all four years. For ten years, he and his brother served as ball boys at local tennis tournaments. He tried his best to soak up all he could, from the pros he met there, anxiously awaiting his turn to one day be in their shoes. He took professional lessons when we could afford it, but the cost of doing what became the norm for serious tennis families was prohibitive for him. We simply could not afford it. He did what he could to improve his game, largely on his own, coupled with solid advice from his loving and ever watchful dad.

Frequently he was asked to be a hitting partner against top ranked juniors by a few local tennis coaches. He used these opportunities to hit against these top ranked juniors as a favor to their coaches all the while eavesdropping on the expert advice that was given to the other player. These environments appealed to Richie. It thrust him further along in the anticipation of his turn to one day be in their shoes.

In his last year of high school, a book was dedicated to Richie. This book recognized him not only for his skills and abilities but for being kind, respectful, and for his polite sportsmanship. This book is stored in the school's media center. During his college search, Richie was blessed to be accepted by three universities that were in different states. Making that important decision was a tough one. His father helped him out by simply saying this: Do you want to be a big fish in a small pond or a small fish in a big pond? There was no further conversation between them about the matter.

After maybe two days, he emerged with his decision and thankfully he chose the former which happened to be one of our local universities. Once again during his four years of college, he served as the number one player. In his sophomore year, Arthur came up with the idea that he should play Davis Cup Tennis for Trinidad.

This tennis tournament is held annually in any designated country between teams from different countries in a knock-out format. It's similar to soccer's famous World Cup that we all know and love. To qualify to be on the Davis Cup team, he needed to compete in matches against the local players. I took him to Trinidad, and he successfully emerged as being picked to join the team. While he was in college, he did this for three straight years and thoroughly enjoyed it. He competed down there in local tournaments against some of the top local players and did very well.

Around this time, he was at the top of his game. He practiced and trained regularly to improve and strengthen his skills and performances. Arthur also thought that it was time for Richie to leave college behind and turn into a professional tennis player.

It surely was a tempting idea but considering that Richie had received a full scholarship at a local private university, after much thought, he decided against it.

Putting school first and playing college tennis not only gave him the perfect opportunity to discover himself, it allowed his game to blossom and it also prepared him for life after tennis. He worked diligently on his decision-making skills and his ability to work well as a team player. It also afforded him opportunities to extend his knowledge of the do's and don'ts of tennis. Richie continued playing college tournaments every weekend and attended tennis practice most days after classes.

Some days, he returned home a little frustrated and disappointed because the players didn't show up to practice their skills. However, his teammates did not regard practice as seriously as he did. Richie was the only one on the team whose dream was to become a professional tennis player. My guess is, they had their own ideas about life after college. Each year, when they held their awards at the end of the spring semester, he was awarded the Ice Man award. This award is given to someone who consistently manages to keep their calm demeanor whether they are winning or losing.

POSTSCRIPT

When we were raising our sons, one of the truths we shared with them was: Trash comes in ALL races so choose wisely! If you choose to deal with trashy people, then do it outside our front door.

One day I was in the kitchen and took the colander to strain some pasta. I showed them that the pasta represents the people they call their friends. Every so often, they would need to "sift" out some of them when they no longer embody their ideals and values and add others into their circle as they go along. We also told them about the old adage that my mom taught us so many years ago that's still so very relevant today:

Show me your friends and I'll tell you who you are.

LIFE AFTER COLLEGE

One of the players on his team had a brother who owned a tennis training camp in Ecuador. He invited Richie to extend his training there and live with him and his family. About one month after he graduated, he left our home for Quito, Ecuador. He spent a month training in that tennis camp before he began his quest of competing in tournaments as a tennis professional.

During his college years, he interacted daily with the players on his team who spoke Spanish and subconsciously, he was "learning" the language. Living in that Latin environment cemented his ability to speak the Spanish language fluently all the while enjoying living with this wonderful family. He nurtured a close bond with their mama and she with him. Sometimes he accompanied her on the bus to the market and willingly soaked in their lifestyles.

Every day, he deeply immersed himself into their culture, food and local dialect of their language. He really appreciated and embraced their daily conversations at the lunch and dinner tables. He liked how the family socialized by holding meaningful banters while they ate and hung out, some serious, but most were lighthearted. After his training, he left Ecuador and was able to spend two years travelling internationally. He competed in as many tennis tournaments as he could in various countries, reaching as far as India. After Richie spent two years on the road, he ceased his international travels and returned home. He used the money that he earned while on tour to buy a house in December 2007—just two months after his brother bought his house. The interesting thing was, even though it was not planned, our sons were both homeowners in October and December 2007.

It isn't a given that because you could play tennis that you had what it takes to be a coach. He was hired by a company that trains new pros with valuable coaching techniques. Coaching was a natural progression for him from being a professional player. He worked as a coach at the Four Seasons resorts around the world. This gave him an amazing opportunity to travel (which he loves) for work as a tennis coach in places such as Hawaii, Singapore, Mexico, Costa Rica, and St. John in the Virgin Islands. These assignments lasted between three and six months.

One night, he went with us to a party and met this beautiful woman who was heading to college in a couple of months. He fell in love, and they married in March 2012. In September 2016, they welcomed a gorgeous little girl and now live just about one mile from Arthur Jr.

Like me, both our daughters-in-law were born in Trinidad. But they grew up in America—I did not. Over the years, some of our friends have remarked that our sons have followed in their father's footsteps. Could it be that they saw certain qualities in me, being familiar and exposed to my culture, that they subconsciously desired the same for their wives? I guess we'll never know.

Today I am proud to say that they're both reputable young men of good character who have experienced stability and strong spiritual guidance within our home environment. They've moved on with their lives, reflecting qualities that they absorbed whilst they kept a watchful eye on our business and social ethics. They are both married and have given us three grandchildren whom we love dearly and of course they're the finest looking ever. There, I said it!!! Arthur Jr. has a son and Richie has two daughters.

Because of Richie's unusual coaching schedule, he sometimes needs to schedule tennis lessons in the evenings and weekends to accommodate the needs of his clients. His wife has always been super supportive and has lovingly stepped up. She has managed to keep their family functioning seamlessly and staying in the flow.

Many of those former years were filled with baseball, dirt bike riding, tennis lessons, golf practice, and tournaments. Finding money to support tennis lessons, equipment, tournament fees and other relative expenses for so many years was quite a challenge. You cannot get noticed for sponsorship or even improve your skills without playing tournaments.

Measuring those costs and his talents was a daily activity for us. It was very time consuming and exhausting for our family. The skills that he learned has resulted in a rewarding, lucrative and lifelong career in the tennis world for Richie. Over these many years, he has guided maybe hundreds of people in the right direction. He has been highly successful coaching tennis and is currently guiding the processes as the Director of tennis at a local Country Club. I have been inspired by their accomplishments watching them while they matured into such gentle, young men who are great providers and nurturers. I am enjoying listening and observing our sons and their dad exchange ideas about sports, their homes, co-workers, jobs, trucks and everyday life.

Every member of my family has elevated my journey to a higher ground because we were all tied to their journey to a higher ground. One of the highlights of my day is how I spring into action wholeheartedly while I am doing things for them. Through it all, we were able to develop and manage a method of dignity and calm. We were able to stay in one mindset while we kept the very fabric of our lives together, and I would do it all over again.

OUR PRECIOUS GRANDCHILDREN

Our eldest is beautiful and has a noticeably quiet, sweet, gentle, and likeable persona about her. She is a very pleasant and easygoing young woman who's trying to make her mark in the world. She has one year left in high school, works part-time, and we are all looking forward to her graduation and post-secondary decisions as she emerges and makes her mark in her life's journey.

We were able to be present for the births of our two youngest and have had the pleasure of watching their growth. Our eight-year-old has morphed in so many ways over the years. Because we live so close to him, we're grateful for the experiences that we've had watching him transform into a very handsome guy. We so enjoy having him at our home especially for a sleep-over. Lately because of the COVID19 virus, we haven't had the joys of having him. Hopefully, we will be able to resume the lifestyle we've grown accustomed to. It's been tough to see him and not be able to hug or get too close to him.

He loves attending car shows with his parents and knows the names and models of most cars. He likes playing basketball and is currently on one of the local teams. He loves riding his dirt bike, listening to music, swimming and is currently taking tennis and golf lessons.

Our four-year-old granddaughter is growing very nicely. She too has morphed from trying to learn to walk to showing us how she could do cartwheels. She loves to pillow fight and attend ballet classes. She can't wait to resume her classes as soon as this virus dies!

She enjoys shopping trips with her mom, singing and dancing to current songs and playing with her dolls. She also enjoys swimming and so far, is doing well, trying to improve her techniques of floating and the back stroke. It's always a pleasure to have her here and now that she is older, we look forward to having her for a joint sleepover with our grandson.

CHILLING

I have developed a life here that's sustainable and fulfilling. I measure my quality of life not by our material possessions but by how much time we give to our family. I was looking for a safe place to love where I would find my full meaning of this life. I have a soulful purpose that has this eternal light which makes us feel that what we have is enough and that we are prosperous in every way.

Nestling on our back porch nourishes my soul. It is an honor, a pleasure, and a delight. Sometimes when friends say they feel like they just need to get away, I think about how blessed I feel that part of my own happiness literally looks like our own backyard and our home. Everywhere I look, I get a thrill and exuberant delight and it makes me come alive. It gives me vitality. Through the years, it has been an antidote to my medical issues. During those trying times, it has surely served me well by providing hours of escape from my aching body.

I am privileged to be in the presence of my infinite "orchestra" in our backyard. The trees and shrubs come in numerous shapes, sizes, colors, and textures. There is a canal that separates our development from another. In the backyard of the house across the canal there is a very large tree. It seems to be about seven feet or more in diameter. This tree forms the backdrop and frames all the trees and bushes in our yard. I call that large tree the base drums.

The verdant hues of the tree clusters capture my every gaze, commanding and stimulating every sense possible. Some trees are the cellos, others the guitars, mandolins, sopranos, cellos, and not to forget the violins. The percussion section is the beautiful shrubs and plants that we have against the fence. The trees don't all sway at once; they harmoniously know when and how to chime in when the "conductor" (wind) commands. This sweet "orchestra" reassures me with intense appreciation and gratitude that soothes my entire being.

I find wisdom in observing my plants as they follow through in their own rhythm. They speak to me in their own language by always telling me when they need to be watered, trimmed, moved to a different location, or even turned around to face the sun. My favorite plant is the red anthurium lily. They are outstanding, and the beauty of their color may last two to three months from the peak of their beauty. Growing up, I watched my mom care for her many anthurium plants in our yard. I now have several plants that carry the richness of her legacy and love.

Most days, I can spend hours listening, watching, and fully enjoying their language as they speak to me. There's hope and cleansing as I watch the leaves flutter in their own melodies, rhythm, and harmonies capturing and saving me from our troublesome world.

Watching how the birds are so wonderfully and craftily made is absolutely thrilling. Like us, they look so different but each one is magnificent and only the handiwork of our gracious God. They continuously fly from one branch to another and from one shrub to another. Singing, whistling, chanting their various sweet choruses, and voicing their thoughts to each other. The black crows have their own unique deep throat chants seeming to talk and sing to each other. Sometimes they pause to "clean" themselves for quite some time then their chants start all over —this too is one of my "orchestras."

The butterflies come in so many varied colors. They are yellow, orange, and black; or orange, yellow, and black with speckles of white. The bees have a buzzing melody of their own, busily pollinating the flowers from one branch to another.

The sky is another of my fascinating objects to behold. The varied shapes of the clouds that appear is an outstanding facet to observe. They are always in motion. Entering, leaving, and hurrying through on their way to another state and country. I wish that we would all slow down and try to live in these moments. We overlook our surroundings such as nature- the plants, butterflies, birds, and trees that surround us.

Most times, we do not take the time to focus on the flavor of our meals and miss out on the distinct flavors only because our thoughts are elsewhere. I choose to watch TV shows that are enabling and enlightening allowing me to reclaim my safe space. My husband is my shining star; I trust him completely. He gives me a peace of mind as we juggle through life's ups and downs. When I am in his presence, I can turn down the volume of the world and rest in him.

I found me, and willingly stepped into God's miracle. At this present time, we have a friendship, passion, and a shared purpose. The best lesson he taught our sons is how much he has adored, cared for, and graciously treated their mother. On many occasions they have overheard how he spoke with his mother and other family members. He has always been respectful to his mom and family members while he thoughtfully searched for ways to help them in whatever way he could.

How I saw my new life helped me to gain a new confidence that I never knew. Arthur's opinion of me, makes other people's opinion of me irrelevant.

Party Time

For about ten years, on the first Saturday of December, we held a huge Christmas party. In the first few years, we may have invited around fifty friends, but it wasn't long before that number grew to about ninety. Our music was provided by a good friend and his wife who were always very eager to oblige. He is very passionate and versed in his music and has an easy way to connect with the desires of the crowd, keeping their feet and bodies moving in nonstop motion.

This event was an ideal time to jump start the seasonal festivities by renewing our friendships and dancing to the energetic selections chosen by our DJ friend. Our delicious food was cooked by my baby sister who loves to cook and is masterful at it. She's beautiful, independent, ambitious, self-taught and has been able to carve out a fulfilling career path that she's passionate about and enjoys. One month earlier, my sister and I created the meal plan, and I began stocking up on a variety of ingredients that she needed. Our music and food were the key ingredients to the success of our parties.

Each year, accompanied by our precious mom, my sister arrived on Thursday night after making the five-hour drive. She then headed straight to the kitchen to begin her food preparations. She worked tirelessly all day Friday, seasoning up the different meats and seafood as well as chopping up vegetables for the various dishes. On the day of the party, she cooked for what seemed like all day. She methodically cooked every dish, only pausing occasionally to taste and dance a little to our precious soca music. Watching my sister gather and prepare the ingredients while she cooked, was impressive, pure joy and admiration. She made what could be a hectic task seem super easy. She took the guesswork out of everything she touched yielding only successful results.

Her level of simplifying this task is moving and inspirational as she immerses every element of herself into each dish. To say that every dish was tremendously tasty is a huge understatement. These dishes woke up every sensation of taste that you possess. Her cooking became a crowd favorite and quickly became one of the reasons why our friends came back year after year. Unlike me, she knows exactly what she is doing, enjoys every bit of it and every dish turned out to be outstanding. In fact, before she headed home, she was already planning her return and looking forward with utter willingness to once again give it her all.

While we took care of the food, Art worked tirelessly by removing some of the furniture to create space for the "dance floor." He ensured that the layout of the patio area was orderly by strategically placing chairs, tables, plants, and seasonal decorations. He also set up the bar area by the pool making sure that there was an ample variety of drinks to satisfy the taste of our guests.

Our mom was an integral part of this celebration and looked forward to it very much. On the night of the party, after she got dressed, she sat in our living room and greeted everyone as they entered our home. Even though she was not able to join us on the dance floor, she enjoyed the music and talked about the songs she particularly liked. She stayed awake the entire time until the last song ended before going to her bed.

☙

My life during those years, was very meaningful to me. I ran to it and it changed me forever. I released toxic thoughts and chose to be nurtured in the safety of my new nest. It helped me tear down my walls of what I thought family life was all about. Somehow, I knew and believed that I had the power of choice and to lose that, I would most definitely lose myself. I knew that I had something worth fighting for and was willing to do whatever it took to keep it. I am most proud of the chemistry that we've maintained and still enjoy. I am very grateful for this calm, soothing and loving environment that we've created in our home.

The evolution that occurred within me has definitely been a gracious process. Art and I have woven our own impenetrable and stable unit. There is us and then there's the world. Experiencing the love that I have nurtured for my husband and sons has allowed me to become more confident, secure, and the best mom and wife that I was meant to be. I committed my life to uplift my family in every possible way. Because of those quality moments that I spent with Arthur's brother, it unknowingly crafted, transformed and prepared me to meet Art, thus enabling me to connect with his soul quickly and easily.

Meeting Art that first night was a gallant entry into something much greater than I could or even try to comprehend.

As I look back at my life today, all I see are amazing victories. My gratitude list looks like a beautiful Infiniti pool as I savor so many moments of mindfulness.

Trinidad Carnival

Yes, Carnival is that piece of madness my professor alluded to many years ago that I did not know I had. The diversity of our twin islands results in a melting pot of various cultures. The beats and rhythms of our soca music creates enthusiasm, free flowing adrenaline, and plenty exuberance. Thousands of colorful, glittery, and insanely printed costumes are a sight to behold and are one of the main attractions of Carnival. It's a once in a lifetime experience to watch elaborate costumes fused with many different aspects of our local cultures and to witness our steel band performances. This is one of the most exciting ways to feel the true spirit of freedom.

THE FETES

The festivities of our beloved Trinidad Carnival begin just before Christmas and kick into high gear right after. There is an array of cultural competitions, boat rides and fetes at any time of the day. Every one of these fetes is at an all-time high energy and draw massive amounts of people soaking in the latest soca tunes and performers. In addition to a DJ, there's live entertainment by all the top soca artistes who never fail to deliver strong performances of a lifetime thus driving the crowds into a wonderful adrenaline frenzy. Some of these fetes are held at waterfront and beachfront venues with views to die for. These locations are spectacular, breathtaking and create cherished memories.

Carnival evolved from the French who occupied the island for many years and naturally brought their cultures with them. One of their many traditions was holding masquerade balls also referred to as fetes. People who wear Carnival costumes are called masqueraders. Over time, this word has been shortened to "mas." If you wear a Carnival costume, you would be dancing (chipping) through the streets with friends "playing mas."

A fete is a local term once again derived from the French and is used to describe a massive party any time of the year. During Carnival, thousands of people gather at enchanting and picturesque venues that could be waterfront, a beach, a huge hall or someone's backyard.

The many all-inclusive fetes are extremely impressive, over the top, popular and well attended. When you enter, you will always be greeted with a welcome drink of some sort, a bandana, a large cup, or even a bag with an assortment of makeup must-haves. There is a lavish variety of unlimited popular types of alcoholic drinks made with premium alcohol. There's food, non-stop music from top DJs, live performances and loads of beautiful people stylishly and tastefully dressed in trendy fashions.

One of these all-inclusive fetes that we absolutely love to attend is held in the yards of four houses that make up a cul-de-sac. There are several tents erected on their lawns and each house caters to a different category of food so you could stroll from one to the next and indulge in the drinks, food, and desserts at your heart's content. Every one of these tents offer irresistible invitations to enjoy the gourmet delights of our local cuisine as well as dishes from countries around the world. To provide the entertainment, a huge performance stage is set up in the backyard of one of the houses. Just writing about this truly makes me wish that I could be at one of those awesome all-inclusive parties right now.

A party can be a social, laid-back event with pizza and beer and no dancing. Some parties may have a DJ playing music just as a background thing but usually the people would just be chilling and very little dancing. These types of gatherings are nonexistent and simply unheard of during our exuberant Carnival. If that's what you are used to or are looking for that here, don't even waste your time. The level of high energy generated by the many musicians, artistes, background dancers, and front-line singers fuels the audience by keeping us moving non-stop for hours. Sometimes they command our attention by getting us to do the craziest but fun things with just a simple command or hand movement. Chipping down the streets to a soca artiste, one of our steel bands, or DJ music is an awesome and unforgettable experience. Unless you are in it you just won't understand this phenomenon.

Promoters invest a lot of time, effort, and organization when choosing their venues at many various locations. Their main emphasis is to offer the best ambience, easy to get to, ample availability for parking, and most of all, an unforgettable Carnival experience. They use social media, radio, TV stations and mass e-mails to inform the public. Each year, they go all out in their attempt to set their fetes apart from the rest by attracting more attendees. There is always a plethora of people, lots of them professionals like doctors, lawyers, nurses, and judges who lose all inhibitions and have the time of their lives. There is no racial discrimination and no fights; it's all about hanging out with friends and family and singing and dancing to our beloved soca.

Trinis have been described as "insane party animals" because we spend Carnival drinking, dancing, and liming (the local word for hanging out). All day and all night, there are plenty of events, pre-and post-fetes, competitions, and sublime areas where one can take in views of the capital city while sipping and chatting. During the week before Carnival it's totally feasible to attend three fetes in one day—breakfast, early afternoon, and a late-night fete. One's biggest dilemmas can come about when trying to decide which fete to choose.

Thousands of our locals, expats from around the world, and visitors head mostly to our nation's capital city to experience our highly anticipated event. Some of the fetes start around four (4) am, and as the sun makes its appearance, the water trucks begin hosing down the crowd driving them into a wild frenzy. The DJ's pump up the music even louder. The artistes rev up the crowds and energy and adrenaline go through the roof. Controlling one's waistline is a thing of the past—It is a passion that most of us have in our blood. It is who we are.

To enjoy our Trinidad Carnival, we usually arrived ten days before Carnival Monday and Tuesday to enjoy the fetes, pan yards, limes, and shows. By this time, the whole country is buzzing with adrenaline giving rise to an electric infectious atmosphere as people attend the abundance of fetes and various other activities. Believe me when I tell you, that there's always something to do and somewhere to go for everyone. This is not the place to be bored, it's a stress free and unforgettable experience that surely leaves you wanting more and wishing that it would not finish.

Every year I am always in awe at the spectacle of Carnival. I continue to marvel at the amazing creativity of the décor, foods, and musical genius of the various artistes at the parties that we attend. Trust me they know how to embellish tastefully based on the chosen theme for that year.

The colors can either be very vibrant with amazing blends of colors or soft and soothing. Different food areas are embellished to echo the category of food available as they strive to appeal to our every sense.

When it comes to the entertainment, our Promoters definitely know what we need and always provide popular performers who never disappoint by putting on a terrific and praise-worthy show. Most of the fetes provide a Cool Down zone that is furnished with white sofas and white transparent curtains strategically draped very elegantly accompanied by a cool fine mist to soothe your soul. When you get to Trinidad, a good night's sleep quickly becomes a thing of the past. Sleep is not an option. No sleep quickly becomes a reality (that's not what you came here for).

There is way too much to do and places to go. Everything and everyone comes alive. These fetes, various competitions and other events go on non-stop. Carnival week is like an endless marathon and some people appear like they are beguiled as they absorb the joyous vibes of soca music.

CARNIVAL BANDS

Our wonderful soca music is only one of the many aspects of our Carnival. For most people, Carnival is all about costumes. The band leaders spend the year designing, creating, planning, sewing, and decorating the costumes that are beautifully crafted and made to represent their band. The themes are thoroughly researched; fabrics and beading are selected. Wiring and welding are put in place to construct the various components that create all the vibrant artwork that must be lightweight. These costumes, in addition to being beautiful and elaborate, must be made to fit comfortably. They form the colorful parades that are vibrant and not only fun to watch, but are also an amazing experience to be a part of. There is no other freedom like crossing the stage in front of the judges at one of the many judging points along the parade route.

The costumes are designed to depict the theme chosen by the leaders of the bands. Many bands may comprise of thousands of masqueraders. That theme is portrayed by sections that represent the overall theme. In one band, there could be any number of sections distinguished by different colors and designs. When you decide which band, you want to play in, you get to decide which section you want to be a part of. These decisions can be based on price, or which band most of your friends choose. The music never stops at Carnival. You fete, go home, get a bite to eat, shower, get dressed and go to another fete. It's like you are on rewind. We do that for the weeks leading up to our beloved Carnival.

We enjoy visiting the neighboring mas camps to capture the vibes of the themes of the Carnival bands. We enjoy the artistry and beautiful blends of the thousands of colorful costumes and admire the teams who put together so many of the costumes. It's a massive production that is highly organized so that they each are an integral part of constructing the final products. Anyone is welcome to be a part of the many "mas" bands that strive to win the coveted Band of the Year award. Some are large-scale, others medium as well as small bands. The cost usually includes the costume, two days of alcoholic and non-alcoholic drinks, breakfast, lunch and snacks, fully stocked bars, make up stations, mobile bathrooms, goody bags, security, a cool down bus, and on-site paramedics.

Women outshine the men wearing their stunning costumes that accentuate their natural curves—it is empowering. We feel beautiful, sexy and proud as the spirit of Carnival grabs hold of our entire persona. Unlike some countries, everyone can join in with the bands as they come down the streets "chipping" to the sweet and infectious soca beat.

The music is played by the steel bands and music trucks as they arrive playing their song of choice. These are long flatbed tractor trailer trucks that carry about a hundred or more speakers arranged in some fashion and are attached to large powerful generators. The loud music projects electrifying energy making it impossible to stand still. There is no judgment only pure love and enjoyment. Everyone gets immersed in the energy of the rhythms that move through them. It's not unusual to find someone in their eighties chipping down the streets to the music.

It is easy to find yourself making friends with people from all around the world. You could be rich, poor, in between, no one cares, it just does not make a bit of difference. The prime minister and his Cabinet ministers are all a part of this majestic festival and if you look carefully you would be able to recognize their security surrounding them in the streets amongst the people. It's a known fact that Trinidad shuts down during this time, so don't even think about coming here to conduct any business during our beloved Carnival Monday and Tuesday.

Once again, we never took our sons to Trinidad Carnival because it occurs during the months of February and March when school is still in session. The other reason is, we were always playing mas and quite frankly I do regret that—but just a little bit! They saw our costumes while we got dressed at home for Miami Carnival, heard the soca music but never saw us jumping up! We have been staying at the same Bed and Breakfast house in the city for the last eight years. We've formed special and lasting friendships with some of the guests who like us, have a huge appetite for Carnival and return every year to get their fill of this exciting event.

OUR STEEL PANS

Our visits to the pan yards have been a high priority and always an enormous treat. It is a refreshing delight to watch the different races and ages of the musicians. They consistently show up to practice for our very popular and dearly loved steel band competition we call Panorama. This talented competition draws huge crowds of both local and international supporters who religiously follow their favorite band of choice.

There is a unified rivalry that occurs amongst the top steel bands. They work tirelessly arranging their song of choice to sound the best before they go on stage to compete against each other. On the night of the finals, they all have high hopes of scoring the highest points in front of the judges and emerge as the winner. Everyone is on an ultimate high as we get happy, anxious, and a little nervous because we all want our favorite band to win. It's an undoubtedly unique, festive, and joyful night when we all meet to support our band of choice before they go on stage to perform.

Even though I was born there I still find it amazing that these oil drums could be tuned and prepared so professionally, causing the whole group to sound just like an orchestra in the western world. Watching them practice the same piece over and over until they get it right has taught me that this is an utter commitment they make to this musical genre that they love and are very proud of.

One aspect I have admired and appreciated is meeting and getting to know some of the young Caucasian players who usually are in college at that time but come to our lovely island to be a part of the steel band competition. It's always a very fascinating story to listen to their reasons for coming there and more importantly how they found out about Carnival in the first place.

Strolling down Ariapita Avenue is always a treat because it's one of the hubs for everything. During Carnival season, the street is lined on each side with many temporary food and beer stands. All the restaurants and bars are blasting soca and we're always sure to run into someone we know. We could hang out for hours there because there's food, music, and people—that always equates to FUN. Even when the vendors are preparing food, they are celebrating by dancing to soca. It's a time when everyone gladly trade in their troubles, stress factors, and worries. They receive joyous and energetic days having a good old time jumping up with friends in the streets to the sweet, pulsating and infectious music we call soca.

We have a group of friends from the South Florida area who, like us, return home for Carnival every year. One of them own a condo in the heart of the city and head down to Trinidad right after New Years to enjoy the many competitions and festivals before Carnival kicks into high gear. Because they are able to head down there so early, they have been very helpful in attaining tickets for us and getting recommendations from the locals about the best fetes to attend. Over the years, their help has made it so much easier for us to move around. They have also been super amazing at picking us up to attend these functions. One of my favorite competitions is watching the kings and queens of the bands portray their elaborate costumes in front of the judges. These costumes can sometimes weigh over 200 pounds.

The focus of the designer and those who build them must be comfort and the ability to carry it freely. The masquerader must be able to comfortably "dance" the costume with ease to our melodic soca. Points would be deducted by the judges if the mobility of the costume is not supported properly.

At this show you see amazing creativity and artistry at its finest. Sound effects, lights and fireworks are sometimes built-in to the costumes to create moments of wonder, delight, and that ultimate level of excitement. On Carnival Monday and Tuesday, these massive costumes create a photography frenzy when the crowds see them coming down the streets.

On Carnival Saturday, we celebrate "kiddies Carnival." The streets come alive and are transformed with numerous music trucks that accompany the children who have a parade of their own that tends to mimic the adult parade on Monday and Tuesday. They are simply the cutest ever as they're beautifully dressed in such creative and vibrant bursts of colorful costumes. These beautiful children sing and dance their way through the streets to their beloved soca music before they take the stage for this much anticipated competition. It always seems highly organized, and energized. My Carnival experience would be incomplete if I wasn't a part of it.

Thousands of adult spectators show up to encourage, embrace, and marvel at how these children enjoy dancing. Like the adults, they too claim the streets and the stage portraying their different themes in front of the judges as they compete to be the chosen winners. This festival has always been an overwhelming favorite for us. The ultimate goal is to pass on this amazing tradition to our young ones.

ON THE ROAD

Early on Carnival Monday morning—if you are lucky to be asleep, we're usually jolted out of our beds around 4 am by the sounds of our beloved soca blasting from the music trucks as they announce the start of this grand spectacle we call J'ouvert. It is customary to go to a fete on Carnival Sunday night and end up in the streets in the morning partying some more, even though you haven't had any sleep at all.

Carnival Monday starts around 11am when masqueraders display a small representation of their costumes, they save the best for last. On Tuesday, everyone waits in great anticipation to either participate in or watch as each band parades down the different routes. The masqueraders proudly show off their bold, sometimes glittery, creative, and very colorful costumes as they flood the streets dancing to the most popular soca songs blasting loudly from big trucks outfitted with every musical instrument you could think about.

If you are uncomfortable watching people who wear skimpy clothes during Carnival, all those inhibitions go out of the window. You will see all types of body shapes and colors as everyone without exception are fully enjoying themselves. Masquerades receive food and drinks that are usually provided by each band. One of the trucks in the band is usually loaded with all the toilet facilities and every sanitary and personal item that you can think of. The organizers try to think of everything that you might be in need of while enjoying the melodic pulsating sounds. When they reach the stages at the judging points, everything shifts into an even higher energy when it's their turn to jump up on the stage in front of the judges.

This experience is like none other and one must be involved and present to understand the frenzy, adrenaline, and emotional rush one feels. This feeling is impossible to capture in words and I hope that I am not failing too miserably at it. Everyone is captured in an unimaginable and magical feeling and all the stress, inhibitions and distractions, and really any cares of the world, cease to exist.

The music trucks are massive and usually have the soca artistes performing live on top of the countless numbers of speakers that are strategically arranged, strapped, and secured very carefully.

These trucks are an integral part of the parade to entertain masqueraders and the spectators. The streets are transformed into a kaleidoscope of feathers, sequins, and the heart-pounding rhythms of soca. Usually when a popular artiste is performing on top of a truck, the crowds (including me) go nuts, and we get swept up in a wild and energetic frenzy. Percussion groups locally referred to as rhythm sections are also included on a truck to accompany and enhance the beat of the soca music. Oh, my goodness, those rhythm sections play their heart out and are one of my favorite aspects of Carnival. I really wish Carnival had no end! But unfortunately, it does until the festivities return again.

Oh yeah, shortly after we return home, I begin searching for flights for the next year! Witnessing all the creativity of the various costumes, enjoying the loud music pounding out of those trucks, meeting up with friends, having a drink here or there—I am in paradise. Friends, it always, always, leaves me a little sad and wanting more when it's all over. It is not hard to see why I feel that way. In my lovely island of Trinidad, we have a local word: "moreish" meaning it tastes so good, I just want more.

During our first year of living in South Florida, we attended Miami Carnival and before it ended, we both knew that we wanted to be involved instead of just being a spectator. For twenty-plus years we both played mas each year and enjoyed every bit of it. About midnight on Sunday night following Miami Carnival, we returned home completely exhausted, but feeling thrilled, totally exhilarated, and ready to do it all over. During the many years that we have lived in South Florida, we've made a lot of friends from many countries of the world and some of them are still very close to my heart.

COUNTRY COOL DOWN

Each year after Carnival, my cousin took us to visit my father's sister, our Aunty Ellen. It became a special date that we made happen after Carnival. At ninety-four, she was still blessed with an amazing view on life and inspired me every year that I spent some much-needed quality time around her. My beautiful aunty lived a very simple lifestyle in the country area only visiting the city when it was really deemed necessary. Since I did not grow up around her, those visits gave me a splendid opportunity to strengthen our family ties. She was a very gentle soul who spoke softly and moved about quite elegantly, smoothly, and easily. One of the many highlights of our journeys there was when she told us jokes and sang calypsos. I think that the highlight of her day was sharing with us whatever fruits and vegetables were ready for picking. She knew when they were ready by a simple touch of her hand.

Our trip there was always a gratifying one enjoying and appreciating the vastly different landscapes of the countryside. It's quiet, the air feels clean, and we embrace the sounds of the wind through a clump of trees, the various chirping of the birds, the sounds of insects and the barking of dogs as you approach a house, etc. We never feel rushed and there is no blaring of horns to move out of the way or drive faster.

This rustic environment allows us to hit pause and it's an experience that I wish everyone should have. It forces you to "breathe" while you allow yourself to view the backdrop of nature with gratifying lens. These country folks seem to know each other and are exceptionally helpful if you stop to ask about people who once lived in the area. Unlike city folks, they embrace strangers and do not feel threatened by them. Most of them are farmers and chose to live in a rural environment. Once again, I could only dream that one day, the simplicity and joy of life that we were meant to enjoy would return. I wish that the feeling of always wanting more and feeling entitled to more, would just evaporate for good.

Another after-Carnival treat that we look forward to is staying at the home of a very dear friend who is like a son of ours. His gentle, personable, and caring personality is encouraging and makes you want to spend time in his presence. Before I left to get my education in London, we lived next door to his family. I am around ten years older, so we never spoke but I do remember watching him play with his younger sister and brother in their yard. He is the same age as my younger sister, and they grew up as close friends.

About a month after she came for our wedding, he visited and stayed a few days at our home in Virginia. That visit has resulted in forty-plus years of a remarkable friendship. Over the years, we have developed a strong mutual affection with him. We consider each other family. He is handsome, kind, intelligent and it's such a joy engaging in conversations with him.

After Mom moved to the US to be with us, he became a valuable asset to our family. He assisted her by overseeing her financial and other matters relating to property management in Trinidad. Once again, time goes into pause while we allow quality time with him to be of paramount importance.

Florida Atlantic University (FAU)

I have been privileged to have been able to work for ten years at our local university which actually came about in quite an unusual way. Several years ago, we grew fond of the pastor and his wife at our local church and one day, we invited them to have dinner at our home. As usual, the guys began talking about sports and such, but his wife and I talked about our families and work experiences.

About two weeks later, after our church service, she asked me if I would be interested in being a part of her office at the university. My response was "Not really." I was quite happy at home and really was not looking for a job. Two weeks later she sought me out after the church service and said that she had spoken to her boss about me. She wanted me to come in for a job interview any day and at any time that I chose! Art sensed that I should check it out and encouraged me to pay her a visit.

She began the interview by asking if I had a son called Arthur Jr. She then began to tell me the story of her encounter with him. While he was in middle school, she was a teacher there. She was making plans to host a fashion show at the end of the semester and had asked him to be a model, but he refused—no surprises there!! Apparently, she kept on encouraging him and finally he accepted. Since she was familiar with him, I guess she felt she knew me and to my surprise I was hired on the spot before I even filled out the job application.

I worked in an office that provided various cultural events designed to uplift and teach both students and staff about removing any cultural barriers that they may have biases about. The university had such a deep, diverse population and each event empowered us to look within ourselves and make conscious choices to change the ways we generalized about other people's cultures. Several months after I began working at FAU, it was graduation time. My boss had an extra ticket and asked me if I wanted to attend the next scheduled graduation ceremony—and of course I accepted.

I had never ever attended a college graduation, so this was a big deal for me. As I sat there watching the graduates dressed in their caps and gowns, walking into the auditorium to the song "Pomp and Circumstance," I found it very touching even though I did not know them. I became a little emotional and was proud of them for putting in a lot of hard work that had finally paid off. Graduation is one of the best reasons to celebrate because it is an important milestone to achieve.

During this time, Richie was in his final weeks of college and his tennis team had done exceptionally well in tournaments during the year. They qualified for a place in the finals of the very prestigious intercollegiate tennis tournament. They had made it to the finals! This was the first time ever, in his school's history.

This collegiate championship is held annually in May and the dates co-incided with his school's graduation. Some of the team members wanted to compete in the tennis competition while others wanted to attend their graduation. They decided to leave the decision up to the captain (Richie) to make the final decision.

Rich discussed the pros and cons with his dad and on his own, decided against attending graduation. He felt as though most of his team really wanted to experience the joy of winning this tournament for themselves, their team, and their school. The finals were held in Arkansas and the team flew out to compete in this competition. They left with high hopes of being crowned the winner of the NCAA Men's Tennis Championship, thus thrusting their school to the top position of the ranking system. Consequently, we made no plans to attend his graduation ceremony.

On my walk back to the office, I began thinking that if I could watch other people's children graduate, why shouldn't I attend my own son's graduation—just to hear them call out his name? I remembered that his school's graduation ceremony was scheduled to be held in just three days but did not know the details. I researched information on his school's website and found the name of a contact person regarding graduation. When I asked if it was too late to get tickets for his graduation, because I wanted to hear his name, I was rendered speechless at her answer.

She shockingly said that since the students were not going to be there, they would not be calling out their names. I was stunned and speechless for what seemed like minutes. When I regained my awareness, I asked if I could make a suggestion in case this situation happened again in the future and she was very open to hearing it.

I proposed that when a team decides to forego their graduation with the intent to represent their school in any honorable championships during graduation, that it was a meaningful and selfless act on their part. While they're conferring degrees, the school should provide a statement explaining their well-intentioned absence. By doing so, the students would be given the recognition that they deserved when they called out their names prefaced by: "The following students are eligible to graduate but have been successful by reaching the finals of the NCAA men's tennis tournament, scheduled at the same time of graduation. They selflessly chose to represent our school with high hopes of making a much-craved name for our University and unfortunately are not present."

I ended the conversation by not expecting any resolve. In about an hour, I received a call from her with some startling, unexpected and exciting news. She had spoken with the provost, who was unaware of this situation. In her presence, he immediately called the coach and told him that he should do whatever it took to bring back the students for their graduation! She also took the initiative to reserve three tickets for us to attend the ceremony that was only two days away. The school made available the caps and gowns for every student and took them to the Hall where their ceremony was being held. Those students literally came from the airport to the hall and were able to experience their college graduation.

After their grand ceremony, the entire team huddled together in the lobby rejoicing in this glorious accomplishment. I stood in awe as I watched their families rejoicing at this happy occasion. Because their families all came from international countries, they had booked their airline reservations and hotel accommodations several months before they reached the finals of that tournament. The players nor their families never found out that they would have been attending the graduation without hearing the name of their child!

೮೨

During my time at FAU, it has been a one-of-a-kind experience as I bonded with students of so many financial and ethnic backgrounds. I have formed many lasting relationships that have flourished into attending their weddings, christenings, etc.

My closest relationship has been with one of our student workers who was seeking his master's degree. We shared a lot about the similarities and few differences in our cultures and lifestyle. He has met every member of our family and we have embraced him as part of our extended family. He has moved on with his life and is doing very well mastering his parenting skills by using all the morals and values he learned from his marvelous parents. We are still connected through our thoughts, occasional visits and phone calls.

I've learned so much from our students and I believe and know for sure that once again my life there at FAU was planned out (not by me) to include these remarkable young adults in my life's journey. I am very proud to say that they have all in their own ways inspired, stirred, and most importantly, encouraged me. I have grown culturally trying to view life from a different perspective through their much younger eyes.

೮೨

One day, I represented our office by attending a workshop designed to inform International students of the services that we offered. At the end of my presentation, I invited them all to visit our office. A few hours later, two of those students who were from Sri Lanka paid me a visit. That was the beginning of an extraordinary experience as Arthur and I embraced and extended our hearts to them as if they were our own. Soon after our relationship began, they began calling us Mam and Sir.

They had only been in the USA for one month when we met them. Being exposed to our culture was quite an unfamiliar and, in so many ways, a very shocking environment. They were both quite shy and reserved, as they tried their best to interpret what we did and said to them. Arthur did not work at FAU but to support me, he came on campus to attend events with them on several occasions. Sometimes he picked us up to have lunch off campus or to take them to the mall. We both feel bountifully blessed for being given those opportunities to extend our love in many ways during a time when they both needed it.

It broke our hearts when one day, we were visited by the both of them with some rather sad and disturbing news. We learned that at the end of the semester one of them had to return home to her country because her parents could no longer afford to pay for her college expenses. They told us that her family had borrowed all the money that they possibly could to support her tuition, housing and daily needs and could no longer afford to pay for her much-needed education. She was an ambitious, beautiful, and intelligent young woman who desired to provide a decent livelihood for herself and her family and because of that almighty dollar she was unable to get her degree.

The fact that she was an International student was an unfortunate circumstance because the college tuition is much more expensive. We truly were at a loss at the idea of losing her and wished that we could do something to prevent this circumstance. At that time, we were not financially equipped to take care of and sustain the demands of her education. We gathered whatever clothes, shoes, and other goods we could, packed a box and visited with her one last time.

Mere words could hardly describe how much we felt that we were abandoning her. It's really an unbearable thing to even think, let alone talk about. We handed her the box and some cash and after many hugs and tears we sadly departed. That was the last day that we saw or heard from her. My fervent and constant prayer is that she was able to somehow find a resolve to further her education. We can only hope that she is doing well and has as good a life as possible. She will always be in our hearts and if an opportunity arises for us to hear from her, we would gladly do so.

ↄ

I have been able to naturally connect with one of my beautiful and courageous students in her life's journey. We met in her freshman year of college and I became her mentor. It was not what I did but how I did it that effectively transformed and molded her life in some aspects. I have helped her through important conversations by merely listening intently to find any thread that would help her to connect and thus make the best decisions that would be most beneficial for her and her family. My time spent as her official mentor offering guidance and virtuous caring has been one of my many life's triumphs. From the very beginning of our affiliation, this young woman mattered and was valuable to me.

She had an incredible and insightful story of her ancestors that I sometimes could never fully fathom. However, I always opened my heart and drank in every story that I heard while I tried to see the good in her. I embraced each opportunity of listening to her spirit to find her joy, sorrow and most importantly her intention.

I encouraged her to realize that those "someday" dreams were now. The tools she was receiving during her college experiences were preparing her to ask and negotiate for what she deserved and most importantly was worthy of receiving. I used those opportunities to caution her about not allowing anyone to devalue her self-esteem or tell her what she couldn't or shouldn't do. She must never set aside her principles for anyone. She should find the courage to ask the tough questions and implement changes even if it meant putting her privileges on the line. Today, I'm most proud and ecstatic to announce that she's riding the waves of success, having attained the one academic goal she had in mind when we first met—her PhD. I have no doubt that she will continue to accomplish even higher goals in the years to come.

Whenever it was feasible, I tried to elevate and promote internships that were relative to our students' majors. I encouraged it whenever I could as a means of enhancing the purpose and practicality of their field of study long before graduation. If not done, this might prove to be counter-productive when they began working in those chosen fields after graduation.

We always looked forward to receiving our on-campus invitations from various organizations and clubs as they celebrated the end of the school year. They held fashion shows, parties, award ceremonies and many other wonderful events. Even though Art did not work at the university during these years, he always found a way to show up for me as we both soaked in these incredible moments.

One of the events that we always delighted in took place the night before their final exams began. We went back to campus from 8 pm to 11 pm to serve late-night breakfast to our students. They all got a kick when they saw us serving them. For us, it was delightful to cheer them on and offer some encouraging words to help soothe any nervousness. The music provided by the DJ and other activities such as massages and games were meant to relieve stress and to relax them before their exams began the next day.

At our school, I learned a lot about embracing people who brought their many different facets of diversity. I am thrilled to say that many of them have returned to visit me, years after they graduated and moved out of state. I can tell you that what I saw and heard sitting and listening was nothing short of quiet admiration. Paying full attention to their stories of their journeys and accomplishments in their jobs is assuring, satisfying and superbly rewarding. These students inspired me to train and mold them whenever I got the opportunity. Being a mom figure was good for them in those times when they needed it. They're out there in the world now making it happen.

LUMPECTOMY

In 2013, I had a lump in my right breast. This lump was diagnosed after I had my annual mammogram. I had no signs nor symptoms and was quite surprised when I got the results of this finding. That lump was surgically removed (lumpectomy) and was thankfully discovered to be benign (non-cancerous)! One week after my surgery, I felt well enough to return to my job at the University. Shortly after, I was able to resume all my normal physical activities. Since that occurrence, I have been having follow-up breast mammograms and ultrasounds every six months.

Our 2018 European Trip

Arthur has a brother who has three sons. About thirty years ago, one of them migrated to Switzerland and married the love of his life and they have two beautiful children. Over those many years, his nephew frequently invited us to visit his family in Switzerland but since we were still working, we were unable to do so. The last time that we saw him was so many years ago, when he stayed at our home in Virginia with his older brother when they were mere teenagers.

One year after I retired, we planned and fulfilled one of our lifelong dreams. Our six weeks of vacation brought to fruition one of our most successful trips together. Since his nephew lives in Switzerland, we used it as our base to travel to five other countries. They were Germany, Italy, Spain, Portugal, and Paris. Before we left, we carefully mapped out the travel dates to each of those countries and I am happy to say—it was truly a dream come true.

Mere words could hardly describe our most impressive and magical journey through Europe. Reading the different road signs, the menus, the signs on various buildings and hearing the languages was like a big harmonious and rather fascinating orchestra. When we visited the homes of our friends I was jolted by the awareness that "big" is not necessarily the best way to live. It made me appreciate what we own even more.

The genuine warmth of the new friends with whom we bonded, could never be fully described, or forgotten. Sharing fundamental values and beliefs with our new friends, left me with the desire to continue being the human part of the word "human being." We blended with a host of cultures and we are blessed and humbled by it all. My adventurous spirit allowed me to thrive and grow vastly throughout those 6 weeks. Every get-together in their homes spoke to us in such loving and spiritual ways.

The vibes we felt reflected being loved and wanted. Throughout every country that we visited. I have asked myself—is our culture the way it's meant to be? Do the others have it wrong? Is our quality of life so much better than other cultures? I needed to satisfy my curiosity, so I asked our friends from each country that we visited, this question—"What matters to you most about your country"? Their responses have been exhilarating, very moving, not surprising, and thought provoking. I must say that the pride and respect for their countries expressed by everyone was inspirational and outstanding. It left me with a warm and permanent impression and a deep wish that I could feel the same.

THE SWISS BROWNS

Switzerland—After our flight arrived in Zurich, we travelled by train to a town called Thun (pronounced Toon) where his nephew lives. It was a one-and-a-half-hour journey that allowed our eyes to feast on their unique terrain. We used this town as our travel base. Our Swiss family received us with warm embraces and kisses as we tried to update each other for the many missing years. One of my fondest memories is when Art and his nephew met for the first time. They hugged again and again with teary eyes for at least five minutes. The many years and miles apart definitely did not soften their loving family ties. It was one of those feel-good moments that unfortunately, many of us do not get that type of opportunity very often.

Thun is a beautiful small town that has their river water flowing through it and all around it. This river water is extremely clean and meanders its way flowing to and from Lake Thun. It appears like a mirror-smooth mountain lake that in next to no time rejuvenated my lifeblood. In the midst of it, there are foaming locks that are impressive and authentic. During the summer months, the residents can use the river for swimming. It has many hills uniquely made up of wooden, stone and even metal steps. Some are adorned with an inviting bench—the perfect spot to just take in a breath of fresh air and enjoy the view of their local castle and the town.

One day while strolling around, we came upon a walnut tree and immediately stopped to crack some of the walnuts that were scattered around its trunk. Oh, the fresh and delicious taste of those walnuts was so different from the ones we buy in the stores.

The Swiss chalets here are incredibly elegant, artistically detailed and every bit of carpentry is intriguing, timeless, enchanting, and imaginary. Wherever you look there are different shapes of windows with many different flower boxes most tastefully done in a variety of styles. They transform the exterior of their homes, with their use of different styles of brackets thus enhancing the curb appeal.

Thun Castle is located high on a hill, in the heart of the city of Thun. It graces the skyline of the town for miles. It is a unique testimony of the architecture of the Swiss culture that's still heritage protected and time-honored. This landmark has a striking form of four peaks that's visible from afar. Its commanding views are distinctively breathtaking as it offers magnificent, impressive views of the mountains, town, and lake. It serves as an asset of national significance. The picturesque ambiance in this town becomes limitless as you stroll around at a leisurely pace. This town is clean and well-manicured everywhere you look.

We attended a cheese festival that was authentic, impressive, and super outstanding. Their cheeses are an all-natural delight on the palate, and I quickly learned that there is no such cheese as Swiss cheese. The street was lined with endless vendors displaying their wares and everything that goes with them. Having read about them and seen pictures, we were able to witness two men playing the alphorn. I learned that alphorns are twelve feet long and today they're mostly used as a musical instrument in many parts of the world. Centuries ago, the alphorn was used as a means of communicating with the sheep herders, who had roamed afar with their flocks high up in the Swiss Alps. This was an unexpected treat that we welcomed and tucked safely into our treasured encounters.

We listened intently, while his nephew and his family described their annual festival called Fulehung ("lazy dog") with so much excitement. This festival celebrates the end of the shooting season and is held over the last weekend of September. Today it's a much-anticipated event that lasts from Saturday through Monday. We were both delighted that we were able to experience this important landmark of their culture.

The Fulehung is the main character who participates in most of the events until the last event which is the closing cadets' ball. He appears in public early on Monday morning to execute the chase through Thun's old town and it's the most popular of his many duties.

On Monday morning everyone gravitates with huge anticipation to the town's central square. At 4 am, the lights of this small town are switched off with the sound of one heavy "thump." Amidst this total darkness, the crowd utters chants, whistles, and shouts of happiness while waiting for the Fulehung to appear. His outfit is adorned with bells and as soon as they hear these bells, the crowd explodes with joy and excitement. This character appears with a stick that has a pig's bladder attached to its end and pushes his way through the crowded streets, hitting the spectators with his stick as he goes by. It is counted as an honor to be hit by this character and some people choose to appear in front of him just to be hit. At the end of his run through the streets of town, he reveals friendlier characteristics by throwing sweets to the adoring crowd from the windows of designated houses.

One of our many visits with our family took us to Bern, the capital of Switzerland. Its urban aspect, outdoor markets, and abundant fountains have hardly changed over the centuries. Their unique sandstone buildings, tram system and towers seem to be softly guarded by those majestic mountain ranges—the Alps. Their wondrous Clock Tower has become the town's famed landmark and graces the town by forming an imposing background. Four minutes before each hour its intricate mechanism sets in motion several figures such as dancing bears and a crowing rooster. A visit to the tower is worth a visit to see the clock mechanism and to enjoy the superb views over the streets and rooftops of Bern.

A large pedestrian street known as the Avenue of the Arches (all the houses are arched) runs right through the town. The ground floor of these buildings is occupied by various types of shops. Albert Einstein was Bern's most famous resident. His figurine could be found on benches in four different locations in the city.

The Einstein house where he lived with his wife and son Hans is located close to the town's Clock Tower. On the second floor of this house, you would find a small museum dedicated to the scientist where documents and writings about his scientific activities are proudly displayed.

The nearby Parliament palace houses the famous seat of the Swiss government. The domed hall of this palace forms a unique and communal architectural focal point. Their Bear Park is located along the beautiful river Aare and is surely worth mentioning because the city of Bern was named after a bear.

The Alps

My first glimpse of the Alps was pleasing, charming, breathtaking, unexpected, enchanting, and most extraordinary. Its views seemed endless as those magical peaks stretched its way everywhere my eyes wondered. They were so varied in shape and content. They are majestic, unrivalled, and simply enjoyable and refreshing to the eyes. To be in their presence is indescribably relaxing and unmatched. This rugged mountain scenery dominates the town of Thun, bathing its spectators with charm and is an all-natural delight. I gazed in sheer delight and was fascinated as we drove for miles and miles past them. It's as if they all knowingly offered everyone simple, sensual pleasures.

Their endless shapes appeared on the horizon seeming to showcase even the tiniest details—how delightful! They are real and in your face. It was as though I was in another world. My eyes danced in sheer delight and wonder at the many jagged peaks. It was an intriguing, pleasurable process filling me with joyful feelings. The Alps offered spectacular sights effectively standing out against the complementary blues of the sky. There was an element of harmonic vibrations that seemed to invite you to connect with all its components. There are peaceful clearings where one can feel at one with all the elements amidst a feeling of well-being. I felt bathed, embraced, and easily connected to its glory.

Those gentle elements could easily soothe away any troubles by granting in return strength and honor. I found myself getting blissfully lost in the rhythms of their landscape as though I was meandering through their foothills on my own.

Germany—In January 2018, we were on a cruise and met a very friendly and classy couple who live in Germany. When Art mentioned that we would be visiting Munich later that year, they excitedly gave us their contact information and asked us to keep in touch. Two months later, while we were preparing for our trip to Europe, we asked them to assist us by recommending a reputable hotel in Munich. They told us that finding any hotels would be impossible since our visit was coinciding with their world-renowned annual festival called Octoberfest and all accommodations are usually booked months and years in advance.

We were honored when they invited us to stay in their home. We travelled from Switzerland to Germany by bus. This bus ride was extremely comfortable, effortless and in no time, we were in Munich. This bus ride added to another one of our memorable European experiences. Our friends were there to meet us at the bus station and warmly greeted us with loads of hugs and kisses. Our first stop was at one of their famous fruit and flower markets.

It was easy to slide into their festivities and settle into immersing ourselves into their culture. It was here that I found myself hooked on one of their snacks. Its main ingredients are dates and hazelnuts and is oh so scrumptious and yummy. Our conversations were exciting and engaging as we gave birth to a wonderful friendship. We enjoyed their hospitality where we were able to learn about and appreciate their traditional meals and lifestyles.

Their breakfast table was an incredible display of a variety of cheeses; salami; breads; homemade jams and jellies; pretzels; mustard; ham; pork sausage; weisswurst sausage; pickles; a fruit plate of nectarines, apples, pears and plums; juice; coffee; and delicious hot cappuccino to wash it all down.

We visited one of my favorite churches in Munich. It had pillars that were lined with what seemed to be grapevines that seemed to suggest the Garden of Eden. The colossal pairs of fluted half-pillars gave them an air of grandeur. Spaces between these pillars appear to function as private prayer chapels. All the backdrops are rich in symbols that look toward the visitors as if calling for humility, peace, love, and reverent silence. In one of the corners of the sanctuary, there were rose-garlanded female figures that grew from some type of tree beckoning us to be kind and humble. I could not help but pause to gaze at a stream of light that radiated through a very tall façade window. It was as though this light was reaching for the sky above and at the same time, drawing us all to pause and give thanks.

We attended their world-famous Oktoberfest which is held in Munich. It is a time when the entire city is encapsulated in their traditional festivities. The centerpiece of this festival was all about endless beer drinking from huge beer mugs, dancing on benches to the polka with your beer mug held tightly in the air, to eating huge salty pretzels and potato pancakes with people you don't even know.

We enjoyed a great variety of music and food at this massive party. Every street was flooded with restaurants serving beer, food and dishing out different types of entertainment. As we strolled through the streets, visiting tents and areas specifically dedicated to kids, it was quite easy to get caught up in the magic of it all. This festival was my own version of Disneyland! The locals wore their traditional clothing with extreme pride and took their outfits very seriously. Their beautiful dresses (dirndls) were an assortment of eye-catching styles. The bodice was tight fitting atop a full wide skirt. I learned that the way a woman ties her apron tells its own story by signifying her relationship status. If she ties it on the left side, it indicates she is single and ready to mingle!

On the day of our departure, we took some time to pause, cherish, and fully realize what a gracious experience we had just had with two selfless people whom we merely stumbled upon on a cruise ship. They found it in their hearts to extend their home to us, thus granting us the privilege to receive an authentic and unselfish visit. We gathered ourselves to say our goodbyes trying our best to see the good in "goodbye." We had grown to love our new friends and discovered many heartwarming and enjoyable commonalities. We met by chance on the cruise and by choice we became dear friends. Sadly, we had to move on, taking the memories we made and using them to help us look forward to our new hellos.

When we left their home, we felt in our souls that we had found two people who were worthy of becoming an integral part of our lives.

Italy—We left Thun with our Swiss family by car to stay at their Italian villa located in a small village called Torrita Di Siena. This village is located in the region of Tuscany, about 26 miles from Siena and 50 miles from Florence. Driving along the motorways, we were framed by the beautiful Alps. In some areas, we had to climb very steep hills to the top of the mountains. The views were out of this world and had us mesmerized. Art hates heights and was "pushing a hole" in the floor of the car while his nephew carefully maneuvered each curve.

At certain points in our journey to Italy, we drove onto a train. This train travels through a tunnel that runs through the mountains for about 30 minutes. It was a good time for his nephew to take a break and rest his eyes from the driving. Because we were in total darkness this was definitely an eye opener. Altogether the drive from their home in Switzerland to Italy lasted eight hours. However, when you are with family, time seems to just glide on by, exchanging our viewpoints, listening to music, singing, telling jokes and even indulging in a quick nap.

Walking through the narrow, ancient, cobblestone streets and alleys of Torrita, you get a sense of the strong local pride, where they all seem to know each other. There is a sense of community where villagers pay close attention when someone does not show up after some time. This town feels like it's perched on a balcony that offers up splendid panoramic, and very memorable views that seem unending. History is evident everywhere you turn. You feel protected and safe.

This ancient village has been spared by the hordes of tourists and remains a haven for its locals. They reclaim their streets and squares in the evenings to sip on cappuccino at their local bars and have lively conversations amidst many familiar faces. Some prefer to enjoy singing out loud or even dance while they stroll through the streets before or after their supper. It is unique and not a tourist destination.

You could lose yourself in the harmony of its landscape that leaves you with an indelible memory. This village is a sheer delight for those who wish to hear only the sounds of the wind, birds, and unhurried footsteps on the ancient cobble stone streets.

It is an oasis of peace in a world that is almost always in a hurry, never stopping to look at the beauty all around us. Dining here imparts a feeling that you are in the home of someone's grandma. It was here in Torrita di Siena that I was introduced to their local version of Pici pasta which really looks like fat spaghetti.

We visited a church called Tempio di San Biagio in a nearby town called Montepulchiano. This church dwells all by itself in a low-level meadow-like setting where it blends harmoniously with the most beautiful surrounding countryside. The views are dramatic, memorable and touches your very soul. Here we saw endless acres of olive and pomegranate trees.

Another town worth mentioning is Siena—a city in Tuscany. We were blown away by the magnificence of their stunning Cathedral. Siena is well known for the Palio. This is an exciting horse race event that takes place in the Piazza del Campo. Our stop here for refreshing snacks allowed me to take in the continuous parade of tourists, all the while trying my best but without much success, to visualize the Palio.

Before we left for our trip to Europe, Art came up with a great idea. He felt that since France and Italy have been known as cities that depict romance, we should renew our marriage vows in either one of them. His nephew was already overjoyed about our visit, but this idea genuinely aligned with his psyche. He encouraged us to have our vows renewal at their villa in Italy. At that time, we had been married for 38 years.

It was here on the terrace behind their beautiful villa, in this delightful village of Torrita di Siena, where we renewed our marriage vows. It provided the best scenic backdrop which was perfect for our special occasion. That morning of our vows, there was this divine offering that rose up from the very core of our souls, guiding us to write our vows. They were all about our love for each other, the life that we had already carved out and our deep heart's desire to continue our already Blessed union.

Our Swiss family bustled about with their own plans to help us celebrate our day—huge waves of excitement reigned amongst everyone! They even surprised me when they presented me with a beautiful bouquet of fresh pastel-colored flowers for my walk down the "aisle." Quite frankly, I did not even think about getting one for the occasion but thankfully they indulged. Art's great niece was the flower girl, his great nephew played an Italian song for our walk down the "aisle" which was so appropriate for our surroundings.

His handsome nephew escorted me to Arthur, his uncle. His nephew, who is a known singer/songwriter in Europe, blessed us with a song called "Always & Forever," made popular some years ago by the band Heatwave. I don't need to tell you that he did a super, outstanding and oh so memorable rendition of that delightful song. We both became emotional during his brilliant and tender rendition of the song. We were both teary eyed. That song has always been one of my all-time favorites, so I was deeply touched at his choice of songs. Reading our vows to each other after he sang, was not an easy task.

I kept on looking up at the sky desperately trying to drain away all the sweet emotions and those happy tears that were flowing. Only the grace of God got us through it! Yes!!!! it was here in this unique picturesque village of Torrita di Siena where we exchanged our fervent vows, recommitting ourselves to our marriage.

After our vows, our family, some close friends of theirs and a very good Italian friend treated us to an Italian feast under their pergola. This included homemade pizza and other tasty local delicacies accompanied by some very good wine. His nephew's daughter and son baked and frosted an awesome, delicious cake tastefully decorated with Swiss chocolate. After they presented us with the cake, they entertained us by performing a dance that they had both choreographed.

I felt grateful and special to be thought of so lovingly. It added a special flavor to this special event, and I feel eternally thankful for all their caring acts. It was a fairy tale day of sheer magic surrounded by our family amidst the breathtaking views of their courtyard. This day was one of the sweetest highlights of our trip.

Rome—Our visit to Rome was nothing short of spectacular. We drank in the rich Baroque décor and illuminated columns everywhere you looked. After many years of watching the architecture of their buildings in movies such as Spartacus, Ben-Hur and The Ten Commandments, these ancient Christian buildings mixed with some modern ones became a reality. To gaze at the Vatican housed in the Piazza San Pietro (St Peter's Square) is welcoming, most humbling, glorious, and incredibly spiritual.

Its mighty and mind-blowing silver-blue dome, expertly designed by the world-famous Michelangelo, tried its best to dominate the panorama. It transmitted a sense of reverence and solemnness that touches the souls of all who gaze upon it. One can almost feel it embracing and receiving all of mankind in one huge hug. I stood in awe, trying to visualize the huge crowds gathering and filling every fragment of this wondrous space in anticipation of the messages that the Pope delivers at Easter and other occasions. What a magnificent sight to grace my senses!

Entering the church, I was immediately struck by how enormous the basilica was. The holy altar, ceilings, staggering columns, windows, statues, various chapels, thrones, etc., are all superb artistic jewels that I feel very unqualified to describe. It was truly captivating, reverent, humbling, and ALL that! Looking up at the ceiling in the Sistine Chapel revealed what may seem like a complex but brilliant expression of scenes once again artistically portrayed by Michelangelo.

The renowned and legendary Trevi Fountain has many mounds of decorated rocks with statues to include water gushing from every section. This fountain is a magnificent feast of architecture. It is one of the well-known top spots for modeling agencies to feature their models. It has also been the host of many movies throughout time. The striking views from the Spanish Steps in the Piazza di Spagna is downright glorious. It beckons you to rest awhile and take in every crumb that it willingly offers.

Our visit to the Colosseum was another majestic sight to behold. Although it was constructed many centuries ago during the Roman Empire, its unique oval architecture stands proud and bold, daring you to compare it with any other amphitheaters. The image of this massive structure seems to "sit" in the middle of the street and surrounding structures. It brings to mind, the historical events that occurred centuries ago when it was a symbol of power for the emperors. The images of gladiators and the hunts of the wild animals came alive.

Spain—Our next visit was to Barcelona for our "honeymoon." Many years ago, we were introduced to a young man who came to our city to compete in a tennis tournament. He is one of the first groups of tennis players who stayed in our home some years ago. Our relationship grew and blossomed over the years and we now consider each other as family. Naturally, we had a greater sense of purpose of sharing and learning about his country.

We were able to visit his home and meet his beautiful wife, two gorgeous children, and friendly in-laws. What a joyful time that was. They all knew about the many different times that he spent in our home (he always referred to us as "family Brown"). It was a very homely and comfortable experience soaking in all that we saw and heard. He was able to show us around his beautiful country.

One day, he took us to enjoy their world-famous paella. It was marvelous, delicious, and "moreish." I had tasted this dish before but tasting paella in Barcelona gave me an all-time high. Its flavor was tasty and extremely impressive. This small restaurant was cozy and felt as though we were in someone's home. It was here where they introduced us to their popular and refreshing horchata drink. It was refreshing, soothing, and tastes much like a sweet cinnamon and slightly nutty flavored rice pudding.

The vibe of this city would tempt you to stay a little bit longer. It's impossible to visit Barcelona without feeling enchanted by the traditional architecture. The buildings seem to offer up spectacular and incredible sights that stood out against a very welcoming and wholesome blue sky. Equally fascinating are the many cafes and restaurants that frame the sidewalks forming such a rich and timeless heritage. Yes, sweet magic happens here. I relished in the feeling that I was at home.

One day we were taken to a restaurant for dinner. Before I entered, my eyes and senses became glued to the delightful tile work around the arched doorway. On each side of this tiled arch, there was a tall bronze vase filled with pastel-colored flowers sprouting out in every direction, so rich in color and detail. The artistry of it all revealed how each tile was skillfully molded to the shapes and colors of each flower. This had to be an intricate and time-consuming task. Not only did they have to place the right amount of paint in the correct part of the mold but once set, moving the tile from the mold had to require an abundance of skills. Each tile was placed exactly where it should be, giving the illusion that it might be a painting. Just thinking about it takes my breath away.

Our visit to Gaudi's La Pedrera was downright breathtaking. He exhibits pure masterpiece in his architecture. The rooftop of this building is no doubt one of its kind. Attention to detail is evident everywhere you look. I yield to an expert to describe this exceptional display of Gaudi—the genius. La Sagrada Familia is also one of a kind and it's one of Gaudi's famous and magnificent unfinished works. The gothic architecture of this church is indescribable. In the heart of the city of Barcelona, it rises like huge needles before your eyes. The dramatic beauty of this massive church inside and out is intense, impressive and unreal.

I was pleasantly surprised by the unexpected façade that held the exuberant and incredibly detailed nativity scene. As you gaze upon it, you must delight in the fact that this was undoubtedly the work of a mastermind. Spending time with our Barcelona family was one of the numerous highlights of our unforgettable vacation. We were once again feeling very grateful and blessed for their open invitation to return to their beautiful city. We left with heavy hearts saying our goodbyes with huge sighs amidst much hope of returning to see their wonderful faces someday soon.

Portugal—One of our friends who is really considered family knew a friend who is from, and still lives close to, the city of Lisbon. When we arrived, he opened his arms and warmly welcomed us. He immediately took us to one of his favorite restaurants where we enjoyed cozido. This dish exploded with a variety of meats that formed the tasty backbone of it. It's a stew with potatoes and an assortment of vegetables. Our days spent with him were richly rewarding while we enthusiastically drank in some of the dramatic landscapes. The picturesque harbor area is exciting and breath taking. As we drove along, I could not help but pay special attention to the landscape of this bustling city. I was able to connect with the many benefits that tourism has not only created but still is such a vital source of income for this vibrant and magnificent city.

In the city of Lisbon, an imaginary boundary links the river Tejo with the sea. There is a bridge named Ponte 25 de Abril (25th of April Bridge). It's a bridge that was built to look like the well-known Golden Gate bridge in California. The real distinction of this bridge is that it has two platforms. The upper one has six lanes for the cars and the lower one has two train tracks. This stunning bridge connects the mainland of Lisbon to the city of Almada with the beautiful river Tejo separating them.

We drove across this bridge to visit the "Christ the King" effigy that stands tall and majestic overlooking this compelling river and charming city. Its open arms beckon us with hope and love as it keeps a vigilant eye on all who draw nigh. It's one of Lisbon's most captivating iconic monuments inspired by a statue in Brazil called "Christ the Redeemer." The inspiring, panoramic view from the very top is a must see.

In their small coastal town named Cascais, the "Devil's mouth" is a jaw-dropping cliff formation shaped like a cave. The huge waves rising from the Atlantic continuously crash violently against it. As we drove to another town called Sintra, I marveled at their pastel-colored buildings all crowned with red roofs.

This was a delightful and welcoming vista to observe and appreciate. I felt the harmonic vibrations of its forests, birds, insects, and other forms of life as we easily strolled through one of Lisbon's parks. We paused frequently in some clearings to simply relax and feel at one with every different element that we sensed. It was a nice touch to relax from our bustling tours and there could not have had a more perfect place.

This feeling is difficult to describe since it seeks to calm all your troubles away only granting us their strengths and virtues in return. It allows us to be mindful and present in each moment thereby allowing us to walk even further along without ever getting tired. One day we visited their Pena Palace that is proudly perched on top of a hill above Sintra. Once again, the architecture and vividly painted walkways was breathtakingly unique, and unlike any structures that I have ever seen. It would not make much sense if I tried to describe what I observed because I'm sure to fail miserably.

Back in Lisbon, we delighted in their world-famous Pastel de Nata simply put—a custard tart that leaves you wanting more. One of the many highlights of our stay in Lisbon was having dinner at the home of our friends' parents. The simple joyful moments of their authentic, Portuguese home cooking were nothing short of sheer delight to our palate. We talked and laughed like we were old friends who had gathered for a "just because" opportunity all the while feeling so at home dedicating our entire mindset to this unique experience. They made us feel as though we belonged.

They shared with us a small glimpse into some history of what their families went through during some troubling revolutionary times in their beloved country. All too soon, it was time to leave this enchanting country, embracing our new friendships and pledging to return some day.

Paris—Oh, what can I say? I think everyone I know either has the desire or has already visited this great city. This is one of the cities of the world where the latest clothing trends are set and is well known as a true shopping haven. It is here in this bustling fashion district, called the Avenue des Champs Elysees, the heart of this city throbs. Fashion and art are constantly reinventing themselves and in this bustling city; they are often linked together. Some of the buildings depict their unique history, culture, and lifestyles.

Paris houses the Arc de Triomphe and it's plain to see how vibrant and unconventional life thrives here. It captures an inspiring atmosphere while giving you an exciting taste of life in this French capital. Our greatest delight happened when we were in full view of the well- known masterpiece called the Eiffel Tower. It seemed to pop right out in front of us as we walked towards it. To say that this iconic monument is a great sight is the biggest understatement you could ever use. It is a most impressive feat of architecture when you are up close. It almost seemed like a mirage. We indulged in our lunch beside the Eiffel Tower which was a joyful honor to behold without feeling one bit selfish but blissfully blessed.

When you are in its presence it is fascinating, impressive and the work of a true genius that commands us to just stand and stare in wondrous silence. It's an infinite worldwide symbol that draws everyone to pause to behold its magnificence. And if a daytime visit is not enough, venture back to gaze upon this majestic structure while it's illuminated at dusk for five minutes every hour.

I was in awe when we visited the Louvre where we were startled by being face to face with the world-famous Mona Lisa with that smile that we all remember. This structure is so easily recognizable and is one of the landmarks of this beautiful city. The art collection on display is startling and a memorable feast for the eyes. The Notre Dame cathedral stood humbly as it seemed to be boasting about its stained- glass windows amidst the astonishing gothic architecture. The decoration of the interior is outstanding and as I gazed upwards at the sculpted roof, it reminded me of a gigantic rack of ribs. The river Seine quietly and elegantly runs along beside it. We experienced travelling on their subway system and were often accompanied by impromptu musicians whom we so readily accepted.

We were determined to not leave Paris without having their world-famous crème brulee. It was everything and then some as we paused to slowly enjoy every mouthful. Since our return, I've yet to find someone to top the authenticity of that flavor. The distinctive flavor of their freshly baked croissants, had me searching for them at every meal. They were fresh, buttery and oh so tasty and I must confess that I really overdid it by being rather greedy! While we were in Paris, we learned that Austria is really the country who gave us croissants, not France, but who cares?

After we headed back to Switzerland, our travels through only six countries in Europe ended. We could not help but notice the orange, red and gold carpets of fallen leaves everywhere. It was a sure sign that summer was surely sliding away soon to overlap with their winter. We could not believe how quickly the time went by. We noticed that the temperature had cooled considerably. Without any hesitation, we knew that it was time to head back home to our warm climate.

Saying goodbyes to our loving family in Switzerland was a difficult feat. Our time together was fulfilling and very much needed. We have a special bond, and their love and caring left an indelible mark on us. Everywhere we went, we were completely enveloped by warmth. We hope to return as soon as we possibly can and travel to some of the other countries located north of Switzerland.

We are grateful for our incredible luck receiving warmth, hospitality, and perfect weather during our visit. Our European vacation was an unforgettable experience having learned so many valuable and teachable ideals about other cultures. It has literally left us with a taste for more of the same experiences and who knows?

Life's Curveballs

In October 2018, I got the sad and unexpected news that one of my sisters was diagnosed with cancer in her right breast. At first, accommodating this new reveal brought a sense of turmoil to my overall thoughts. I desperately tried to find the most effective ways to deal with this new "animal" that had shown up in my family's lives.

My sister was treated with what seemed to me like endless weeks of chemotherapy followed by surgery and radiation. She is now on a regimen of taking a chemo pill for five years. She lost her hair and has had to make many lifestyle changes. More importantly though, currently—she is cancer-free. She is coping with several very painful side effects such as bone damage and pain in many of her joints.

She took care of our mom who lived with her assisting her with meals and other necessary aspects of daily life. Mom was privy to the discomforts that she encountered due to the side effects of the chemotherapy. She had frequent bouts of nausea, vomiting, and fatigue. But somehow, my dear sister was able to find ways to still accomplish daily tasks such as cooking, cleaning, and laundry.

I think that it was an unimaginable and despondent thing for my mom to witness how her daughter endured those daily discomforts. How our mother must have really felt as she watched her daughter suffer through so much uneasiness coupled with the abundant visits for her treatments remains a deep mystery to me.

Direct Impact

In December 2018, I went for my usual six-month scheduled mammogram and after the technician took the films, she asked me to wait while she checked them. When she returned, she said that the radiologist requested that I have an ultrasound of the right breast to render clarity to an abnormality. A few minutes after she performed the ultrasound, she told me that the doctor wanted to speak with me, and she took me to a nearby waiting room. By this time, I sensed that my results were irregular and outside the expected norm. I began to get very anxious and suspicious. My mind began going in many different directions imagining the "what ifs."

As the doctor entered the room, my fears were all too apparent and he assured me that my reaction was normal and that it happens to him all the time. I was then told that there were some abnormal cells and was advised to have a breast biopsy. My entire persona became frozen from this very shocking news.

In January 2019, I had the biopsy and waiting for the results was nothing short of a sense of extreme edginess and disbelief. I simply had to remain extremely patient. Unfortunately, but also fortunately for us, I received a wake-up call that catapulted me out of my normality, and it changed everything.

Yes, I had early-stage cancer cells in my right breast, similar to my sister, and I was advised to contact a breast surgeon. I remember saying to the doctor, "Are you sure?" When you are diagnosed with a disease like that, the word alone conjures up scary conclusions, fears, and terminal thoughts. Mere words could hardly describe how terrified and petrified it was to get that type of call. As I replayed the conversation with the doctor over and over in my head I just couldn't believe that this diagnosis had laid its ugly head on me. I experienced moments of stillness which, in turn, offered me a valid opportunity to reflect in disbelief and confusion.

Arthur was not in the room during my conversation with the doctor. He was getting dressed to meet up with a friend to have some guy time. As he walked towards me to kiss me goodbye, he sensed that something bigger than any of us had made its entry into our lives. From the moment that I told him about my diagnosis, I had no doubt that he would drop everything to accommodate this life changing situation. He did what only my husband Arthur would do. He promptly canceled meeting up with his friend.

Making an appointment with a breast surgeon became my paramount responsibility. Everything and everyone else faded into the distant background.

But on the day that this sickness revealed itself, the winds of change blew stronger than I have ever seen them move. I found little relief as I let out a cry in this earthquake of disbelief, deep sadness, and fear of what was about to go down. In times like these, our daily lives can just stop in its tracks and time then seems to stand still.

SETTLING IN

We had a great deal of confidence in the breast surgeon whom we had used for my lumpectomy a few years ago, and it was a no brainer to charge her with the huge responsibility of my current and much-needed care.

Because this cancer had casually announced itself, two weeks later we were both seated in her office anxiously awaiting the birth of this new phase of our life's journey.

The breast surgeon asked us both to move our chairs closer to the examination table because she wanted to "map out" her treatment and the prevention plan of this disease. On the paper that lined the examination table, she drew an image of the breast and pinpointed where the cancer cells were. She wrote down the 4 stages of her treatment template and explained in detail what every step would entail. It was masterful, it was real, and everything clicked. My treatment plan was: surgery, radiation then a chemo pill for 5 years—meant to effectively prevent any cancer cells from invading my body by metastasizing to neighboring tissues.

Because I had early-stage cancer, thankfully I did not need to be treated with chemotherapy. This doctor handled the visits with preciseness, knowledge and ushered in a remarkable measure of confidence that resolved so many of our questions and fears. We were told that I would be connected to a team of doctors. They would all be focusing and guiding me along with my care based on their areas of expertise of my treatment plan. This priceless team comprised of a radiation oncologist, a medical oncologist, and a psychologist/dietician.

The role of the radiation oncologist was to prescribe the size and type of catheter to be implanted in my breast. This catheter would be used to transport the radioactive seeds directly into the area where the cancer cells were removed. He would also be managing the dosage and frequency of my radiation therapy.

The medical oncologist was to prescribe and manage the chemo pill that would hinder cancer cells from being invasive. I would have to visit her every two months for blood work to monitor hemoglobin, red and white blood cells, and other tests. The role of the psychologist/dietitian was to manage on an ongoing basis, my mental condition and daily dietary needs.

I had to quickly learn the roles of each of these specialists to fully grasp the clarity, requirements, and timelines of their individual instructions. After researching many aspects of my treatment plan, I was able to fully understand my new path to wellness.

This diagnosis has been a powerful revelation.

I had to find in myself, methods to accept this diagnosis and develop a strong fighting spirit. I then lowered myself deep into the trenches of my inner self, stayed attentive, thankful, and consistently prayerful. I decided that I was going to embrace this situation and attack it with a sense of gratitude that the cancer was still in an early stage. I had to summon up every bit of courage that I could fully grasp.

Always having Art present (not only physically) with me was of paramount importance and matchless appreciation. Sometimes based on what I heard, my mind wandered off in many different directions and I would miss some of what was said. But in our discussions after the visit, he was always able to explain what I may have missed. We attended each office visit listening intently to what we needed to do. He understood everything and cared deeply about how I was receiving as well as reacting to it all.

My prognosis provided encouragement and comfort based on a test called the Oncotype DX test. One of my doctor's main thrusts was to inform and advise us about any new developments, or changes to her practices and techniques in the fight against my type of cancer.

My Coping Mechanisms

My consciousness became alive, and an insurmountable amount of courage and faith resounded. This helped me define sound ways of handling all that my diagnosis encompassed. The outcome became clear, and I embraced my own version of tackling my current situation my way.

I reached out to a few selected friends and family members by making some phone calls that lasted one to two minutes. These calls were really a very short monologue and left no room for discussions. It went something like this: "I've been diagnosed with breast cancer. I'll be having surgery in two weeks followed by radiation two weeks later. I'll be out of touch for some time and will resurface when I'm able to." The end!

Naturally, they were stunned but I am grateful that they let me be and were super understanding by not calling or texting. It was the only way I could find that would allow me to focus on the healing that I had already requested from our Mighty Physician. I needed to be able to surrender and be available to accept His healing in His time.

Any negativity, stress, or anxiety from them would disrupt the signals of healing that my cells and immune system were trying to adjust to. I would not allow toxic thoughts or perceptions to interrupt my new healing environment. I did not want or need to experience anyone's life but my own. I had to disrupt and reconstruct my life patterns to not include them. I simply needed to condition myself to get out of the way of healing or suffer the consequences. I set my sights on huge possibilities instead of focusing on obstacles. I had to believe in the magic of what might be.

It would have been so easy to give in to fears and anxiety. Staying in those dangerous and disturbing mindsets could very quickly become toxic cesspools. Submitting myself to worrying about bad stuff would not stop it from happening. All it would do is, it would stop me from enjoying the good that's all around me. These new set of circumstances selfishly became elevated to be: ALL ABOUT ME. I only choose to seek wisdom rather than allow other people's darkness to overcome me. My light must prevail.

One of the characteristics of cancer cells is that they run and hide and sometimes multiply uncontrollably. The goal of the treatment by the chemo pill after my surgery and radiation therapy was to seek and destroy any "runaway" cells. It stops them from metastasizing to other parts of the body thus invading neighboring tissues by traveling to the lymph nodes under the arms.

Picture this. You have a lemon, an orange, and a grapefruit—each of these are different in size. The surgery removes the area where the cancer cells are along with a small amount of healthy nearby tissue (the lemon).

And just in case there were more cancer cells that the surgeon wasn't able to see outside of the areas of the lemon, the radiation would remove them (the orange). The chemo pill would seek to destroy cells that may have escaped and multiplied into other areas of the body (the grapefruit).

I took my nephew's advice who felt that it would be a great idea to use Facetime to keep Mom in the loop with each step regarding my treatments. Since she wasn't physically with me this method truly was a source of comfort that eased her mind.

After surgery she was able to see the bandages over the incision site. During my radiation, I showed her where the catheter was and explained how the whole process worked. She listened intently each time in her usual quiet way and showed that she fully understood and approved of that form of communication.

FACING THE MUSIC

In February 2019, on the day before my surgery (the "lemon phase"), I was instructed to have a catheter inserted into the site where the incision would be made. The purpose of this catheter was to allow the surgeon to inject a dye that would illuminate the cancer cells. This would enable her to effectively remove them. My breast surgeon said that the dye identifies the cancer cells by illuminating all the cells, making it look like a runway.

The night before my surgery, as I was preparing to get into our bed, I experienced some very deep thoughts about what I was about to face. That little voice in my head was telling me that my life was about to step into yet another dimension and that life as I knew it, would never be the same. I resolved to accept the unknown as part of my chosen life's journey and had a really good night's sleep.

Recovery from my surgery was uneventful. Once again, my very wonderful and amazing husband stepped up and made everything happen seamlessly. I believe that the psychological impact of these circumstances is guided by one's unique life's journey. As I've said before, no pity party here; my attitude had to be—tell me what I need to do, and it will be done. It would be much too easy to give in to fears and anxiety and dangerous to stay in that toxic cesspool. I refused to let myself go there. Instead, I found mountains of wisdom within my daily challenges.

At the end of February 2019, two weeks after my surgery, I was scheduled to begin the radiation therapy—the "orange phase." Honestly, I was very terrified and afraid. I was harboring my own thoughts about the damage that this radiation would do to the good cells.

Sometimes I think those horrid thoughts wanted to solely consume me, but I did not allow it. I didn't/couldn't let myself (except for a few moments) go to a really dark place.

The day before the start of my radiation therapy, I had to have a catheter implanted internally as close as possible to the incision site. Based on the dialogues that my radiation oncologist had with my breast surgeon, he decided the size of the catheter that needed to be placed in my breast. He also determined the appropriate amount and frequency of the radiation dosage that I would receive. This form of internal radiation therapy is called brachytherapy.

This catheter would contain the seeds that would be placed in a precise location of the body. The goal is to reduce damage to surrounding healthy tissues. The purpose of this catheter was to deliver the radiation dosage directly into or close to the area of the incision. I had to have it inserted on Friday for radiation to begin on Monday.

Right after my breast surgeon placed the catheter in my body, we headed over to the radiation oncologist for him to double check that it was placed exactly where he requested. My treatment team was comprised of four specialists directed by the radiation oncologist. He made the determination that I would be receiving ten doses of radiation. Each of these doses were delivered in two sessions per day for one week. Each session lasted around twelve minutes. I arrived there at 8:30 am, returned home to rest and have lunch, and returned to the facility at 2:30 pm.

Even though I was able to drive, Art happily drove me to every treatment. As expected, he wanted to be present for me before and after I had my therapy.

At the start of each session, the end of the implanted catheter was hooked up to a machine. It had about a dozen tubes which were attached to my implanted catheter. These thin long tubes that came out of the machine reminded me of spaghetti machines that crank out the noodles after the dough is placed in the machine. While the radiation seeds/pellets were being delivered through these tubes and into my breast, I had to lie still with my right arm resting over my head.

Because this catheter had to stay in place for one week until the end of all my sessions, I needed to wear a specialized bra that held the catheter in place. I was not allowed to wet the upper part of my body from the breast up due to the strong likelihood that the catheter would be nudged from its functioning position. During that week, having a full body shower became a matter of wishful thinking. Rather than becoming all shook up and overwhelmed, I had to make good sound judgments by adjusting my daily personal hygiene routine. I must tell you that not being able to have a full body shower for seven days is an uncomfortable and strange idea to maintain and tolerate. I had to buckle up and face this new facet with a smile.

My radiation oncology team were amazingly attentive and helped me stay positive by cheering me on during each of my visits. From my first visit, I was immediately put at ease by their kindness, years of expertise and knowledge. I felt like they really wanted to be there and were always reassuring me that I was going to be okay.

Part of my recovery was to attend visits with the psychologist. These therapy sessions were supportive and helped me further understand this medical situation. Each time I visited, I had to complete a survey. It related to my current thought process and sleep patterns. She assessed, guided, and encouraged me during those confusing times.

THE AFTERMATHS

I am now in my "grapefruit" phase, taking my daily dose of the chemo pill. I have utmost gratitude for the life I have already had in this journey of life and I have immense peace and joy. I have learned how to feel and appreciate pleasure and I'm very happy that I've been successful in what I've already accomplished in this life by being very productive, caring, and helpful. My family holds the best parts of me, and I will continue to focus on the present.

Today, I have a much different view of my life, having visualized that edge—the one that we are all guaranteed to see some day. In normal times most of us do not allow ourselves to go there, and really, why would you?

Currently, I am coping with some of the challenges of the side effects that come with this chemo pill. So far, it's stopping the cancer from re-occurring but one of the many side effects attacks my joints such as my whole pelvic area and knees. My pain and discomfort may seem unique but it's the same as everyone else's. Pain is a thing that comes out of no-where and won't leave—no matter what I do.

On those extra painful days, there isn't much that I could do to get rid of it. I try to get myself together the best way I can and simply move on—it's just another day!

Throughout those many years (since I was 12), I adjusted to the fact that I've been surrounded by pain ALL THE TIME. This is my terrain—my familiar territory. I thought that I was armed with most of the necessities to survive this but I am still learning to "breathe" and wait it out.

Those joints stiffen when I sit too long and are very painful when I get up. On one of my doctor's visits, I complained about some of these side effects and the doctor swiftly said: "But you are alive, aren't you"? And yes—she was right!!! This brief but relative statement quickly put things back into true perspective with a lot of food for thought! I had some learning to do. I had not yet learned how deep the side-effects run and boy was I in for a rude awakening.

I have also been diagnosed with peripheral neuropathy in my feet and fingers. The toxicity of these drugs has killed off part of my much-needed nervous system and it's progressing. I had a consultation with a doctor to explore treatment by light therapy. This resulted in an out-of-pocket expense of $6,000!

Sometimes I feel as though my insides are quietly eroding. In those moments, I must quickly change my mindset. These brief states of grief and confusion now appear in every corner of my daily life and I must be extra strong to conquer them.

I must choose to live in the present by finding what's good about it. I don't want to lose myself by focusing on what's not right or what doesn't feel good. This makes me feel alive, grateful, and abundantly blessed.

My breast cancer journey is my own and I fully embrace it. One of the hardest parts of it, though—that I still struggle with—is asking for help. I learned to stop complaining about daily pains years ago! Psychologically, this journey has not been and still isn't easy. I have been holding on tightly all the while using every happy moment that I could find to keep my spirits up. I sometimes ponder about my sons and their children. They are now burdened with potential cancer risks in the future.

Pain, grief, and loneliness (even if I am in a crowded room), are harsh sensations that I must endure. They're understood only by those who live this reality. Submitting myself to worrying about the "bad" stuff is not going to stop it from happening. All it would do is, it would stop me from enjoying the good around me.

The information that I got from my research on cancer was great BUT it's different when reality hits. Sometimes my thought process was always probing to find my weak spots, desperately trying to get through to my defense mechanisms. Mentally I don't feel old but physically it's a different story. I have found wisdom within my daily challenges. My positivity helps me take on the new trials that emerge! My storms have come, and some trees have fallen, but I woke up this morning!

I have grown immensely in my awareness of my arthritis and my cancer diagnoses. I control the side effects instead of allowing them to control me. There's no wallowing in misery here and that's non-negotiable. There's life after cancer. Currently, parts of my lifestyle are not the way that I want it, but I'm alive. My positive attitude and willpower will continue to help me achieve as healthy a lifestyle as possible.

One of our very close friends equated these trying times as making withdrawals from my deposits. It's like all my experiences and happy moments so far like my travels, Carnival enjoyment, my happy marriage, our admirable sons, etc. They all became deposits in "my bank." Every now and then when those tough moments show up, I can sustain each day by making withdrawals from "my bank."

Currently, we pay attention to what we eat and staying physically as well as mentally active. Our survival has been based on a true friendship grounded in boundless love. I have chosen to fortify myself with very few people—my core family, my doctors, and a small handful of friends. I only keep those who listen to how I'm feeling. I refuse to surround myself with negativity, gossip, stress, or worrying about why people are or aren't doing this or that.

Yes, this is the real deal. It is the reality of my lifestyle choices today. I am all about focusing on the day-to-day quality and content of my life and not about worldly possessions or comparing myself to others.

I no longer have the energy for meaningless friendships and forced interactions or unnecessary conversations.

I strongly believe that when we are broken there's no reason to see all things as broken. We need to draw from everything that's not broken to help us mend using the best objectives. I am trying to get busy living, by not looking for obstacles. Sometimes that's not easy to accomplish but we must push on. I am making this life happen by believing that everything is rigged in my favor and that I am blessed.

Saying Goodbye

On March 13, 2019, twelve days after I had my radiation therapy, I received the unexpected and unhappy news that my mother had died in her sleep. The sting of her death caught me off guard. That call was one of sadness mixed with joy and gratitude that she did not suffer a long illness. Thankfully, mom survived the lengthy discomforts that come from being paralyzed, bed bound etc.

The morning that I received the news that mom had passed away in her sleep, I was in the process of getting ready for an appointment with the medical oncologist. It was her turn to play her role in the continuation of my treatment. She would be prescribing the chemo pill that I needed to take for five years. This would provide a structured regimen to eradicate the recurrence of the breast cancer.

Despite this turn of events, I still showed up for the appointment. My doctor was extremely compassionate when I told her about my mom. She told me to take care of my family needs and that we would begin the chemo pill therapy after I got through what I needed to do. This was a touch of the type of caring that I so needed at that time. That same day, one of my daughters-in-law was already at the airport on her way to another state to begin a job assignment. Once she heard the news about mom, she promptly cancelled her trip to be there for our son.

My nephew and granddaughter put in some long hours and did an outstanding job putting together a slide show that honored her. It not only allowed us to reflect but to appreciate so many of those joyful and fond moments that we shared together. Their preparation was one of the cherished components that helped soothe us as we celebrated her unique life.

One of my nephews did some leg work on some different choices regarding planning of the final arrangements for Mom. When one of my sisters arrived from out of town, she was very thankful for what he had already accomplished. She was then able to use that information to begin the process of choosing the best options to provide her memorial service.

Mom was the glue that held us together, she was our anchor. She is a person you could never forget. Losing her feels unbearable at times. I have dared to imagine what my life would have been like if I never had her at all. My love, admiration, and respect for Mom has given my life true meaning and will live on forevermore.

Our sons gathered their families together while we made our travel plans to say our goodbyes and honor my precious mom. They were able to rent a large house that would allow us all to stay together. They also decided that they did not want us to drive. Instead, they invited us to ride along with Arthur Jr. and his family and return with Richie and his family. With heavy hearts, we drove to Tampa.

One component that was truly effective for me was the fact that my core family were all able to stay together in the house. That team of support was the vehicle that I used to carry me through those many rough waves of emotions. It made it very soothing to receive.

The task of honoring her memories was simply elegant and beautiful. The focus was not on her death, but on the joy that she brought to us and others. The sting of death caught me off guard when the truth that I had really lost my mom revealed itself by an inner ache that was not ready to be soothed or disappear. In times like these, we find truth in knowing that life and death are entwined in one thread.

My brother-in-law led the service with prayers and shared with us his love and appreciation for our mother. Mom had a special place in her heart for him and I know she listened to his every word. My marvelous husband delivered a genuine and elegant eulogy. Mom deeply loved Arthur from the first day that she met him, and I know that she was pleased.

Some of our dear friends were able to share their thoughts, memories and well wishes with our family and friends who gathered to say their goodbyes. A few of our family members chose to express special thoughts by acknowledging how much our precious mother meant. I choose to honor and celebrate the life she lived. Instead of focusing on the sorrow of her death, I give praise and honor her for her dedication and raising us with love and deep compassion.

In the room where we gathered to pay our respects, there was a special table set up. It displayed some of the items that she sewed and crocheted and were very attractively displayed. There were various colors of doilies and blankets that she made over the years. There was a basket that contained balls of wool, knitting and crochet needles, watering cans and flowers like orchids. It created a graceful backdrop for the perfect final sendoff that helped to celebrate her. I know for sure that she would have definitely approved of this lovely, elegant display.

It has already been two years since our mom has left us and there is never a day where some memory of her doesn't flash by. She has left such a void that no one could ever replace. Mom, I will always miss you.

My Solace

In the early days, weeks and months following her death, I quickly found out that grief was a very demanding companion. It was always there—simmering, lingering, festering. Some days it came like a wave. It would rise up and pulse through me as if it was going to tear my heart right out of my body.

In those moments, I felt like I could not bear the pain for one more minute much less one more hour. But through it all, I knew that when life tries to pull you under, we should always choose to kick against the bottom, break open the surface, and breathe again. I have utmost gratitude for the life I have already had in this journey of life because I have immense peace and joy.

Some of my healing moments come from delighting and finding styles of comfort in my many memories of her and feeling every sense of joyful gratitude because she gave us her all. Not surprising, she was a crucial source of composed understanding and support during those tough months of our treatments. In my solace, I had to maintain a hopeful outlook in those dark moments and find ways of facing my future without her. This sustains and strengthens me when those sad moments return.

Within those peaceful and calm moments, I was able to heal those spaces that only my mom occupied. That secret space that I held for her, is now absent and at times becomes unbearable. Those moments inspired, strengthened and encouraged me to never give up. It was then that I called upon patience, wisdom, and true acceptance in the knowledge that she is in a better place.

CRUISING

Because I love to travel, I have engaged in a few wonderful cruises with Arthur and one of my cousins since retiring. Cruising has become one of my favorite ways of exploring so many incredible destinations. It allows me to pause, inhale, and capture breathtaking views that delight my senses. It agrees with me while I'm relishing in glorious, extraordinary experiences. I can leave behind all my cares and the chores are left for someone else. All that's required of me for the next few days is to shower and change my clothes and I could definitely handle that.

I always experience a sense of wonderment while going through the boarding process. It's a joy to watch the faces of the people who are wrapped up in exciting anticipation. I could feel the electricity promising us great things are about to happen. I use every opportunity to become acquainted with other shipmates while waiting my turn to board. Some folks choose to become stressed out, but the right attitude and preparation go a long way to set the appropriate tone.

My first moments of entering the main atrium of the ship and figuring out the location of our cabin is so thrilling. I look forward to the mouth-watering global cuisine and interacting with a wide variety of people from destinations far and wide. The crew members are usually from all around the world and take pride in sharing their stories. By taking a few moments to talk to them, you get a sense of their humanity and family structures.

The energy, excitement and disbelief at what some folks would do to win a prize during the activities on board, creates such incredible vacation memories. Every day you are pulled into new, and fun filled activities which sometimes present a tricky situation because you want to do them all! The entertainment at the poolside is always one of my favorite places to be. The energy is magnetic and nothing but an abundance of joy.

Going on shore to participate in the tours was always fun but whenever we returned to the ship, it always felt good and comforting as crew members are always outside welcoming us back "home" with a refreshing drink; a cool, wet, washcloth; and warm smiles.

In September 2017, my cousin asked me to go with her on a cruise to Alaska. We had seen each other many times at family functions but never spent quality time with each other. Without hesitation, we embarked on our magical journey of self-discovery that was harmonious. What we learnt was that even though we were miles apart for so many years, it did not change our relationship one iota.

We bonded with each other from the very moment when we met at the airport. During our cruise we found a sweet, spiritual connection that flowed daily like a gentle breeze. There was never any drama, only much laughter and great companionship which warmed my heart.

She's gentle, articulate, intelligent, classy, approachable, warm, and beautiful inside and out. With utmost strength of compassion, she epitomizes how a woman should act. To sum it up, she is a class act! I am happy, proud, grateful, and blessed to say that this amazing connection is still valid today.

The landscape of the Alaskan mountains is majestic, stunning, awe inspiring, boastful, breathtaking, distinctive, spiritual, commanding, relaxing, and yes—it's ALL that! The vast terrain of the mountains parades itself as though the mountains are daring us to find their equal. Some are taller than others and seem to dominate the scenery, but their tapestry excels, thus creating authentic and cherished memories.

We were able to watch whales proudly frolicking and showing off their innate skills, causing my smile to grow in absolute amazement. We also enjoyed watching huge salmon displaying their craft by jumping high out of the water while twisting their bodies as they seemed to be engaged in playful games with each other. We witnessed seals on many pieces of the ice basking in the sun and taking their turn to dive in search of food.

One day we were heading to visit a glacier but before we got too close, a gigantic iceberg had broken off and drifted away with the ocean currents. This resulted in huge chunks of ice everywhere. This posed an impossible and hazardous threat for us to continue our journey. Because of this, the captain had to shut the ship down and very slowly turned it around in the opposite direction to move away from the sea of ice blocking the passage to the glacier. Making the turn had to be a skillful and well measured one because our ship was in a very narrow part of the sea. I must say that we were literally holding our breath while this was happening,

The Alaskan scenery was a wonderful, unmatched experience of mother nature. It was loaded with serenity and surrounded by some peaks that are mist covered. Those moments of awe are one that I could never forget. It marked a special time creating unforgettable memories and spending such quality time with my loving cousin. One day soon I would love to be able to revisit Alaska with Art.

In January 2018, Art and I fully enjoyed our ten-day cruise to the Western Caribbean. We visited places such as Costa Maya, Roatan (Honduras), Belize, the Cayman Islands, and Cozumel. It was a beautifully decorated and clean Italian ship that catered mostly to the flavorful cuisine of Europe. The food was always delicious and had us looking forward to learning more about their dishes at the next meal.

On this cruise, I was captivated by the gracious and elegant ballroom dancing that occurred each night. It was the highlight of my nights and was the most enjoyable feature that I anticipated. I learned that this group of dancers were members of a specific school of dance who sponsored dance-themed cruises several times a year. It was designed for women who either did not have partners who liked to dance, or their partners simply had two left feet. An agency provided male partners who were paid to dance with them. These ladies were identified by a boutonniere on their wrist. The men had to dance with a different woman for each song. It was very elegant, classy, and very tastefully done. They danced to the waltz, rumba, jive, salsa, swing, cha cha cha, and even the hustle. It woke up a deep desire in me and I was overjoyed when Art danced with me a couple times.

In May 2018, I visited the islands of St. Kitts and Nevis with my precious cousin for one week. After we landed, I was overjoyed to find that the airport building did not get "attached" to the plane for embarkation. It was sheer excitement, a sense of "freedom" and joy to be able to step down from the plane all the while absorbing the vibrant, calm, and elegant scenery of this charming island.

Each step that led me from their tarmac to the airport building made me feel rather special and grateful for this rare and unique experience. These islands were unbelievably beautiful, clean, serene, and nostalgic.

While exploring the downtown area of St. Kitts, I was ecstatic to discover this wonderful platform of untouched buildings that took me back in time. It reminded me of how the buildings were in the downtown area of Trinidad's capital city when I was in high school some years ago. They seemed to be blissfully trapped in years gone by and not making any apologies for its retro feel. It provided a complete disconnect from the modern world that I was used to. There were no towering buildings, and no fast food restaurants to remind me of where I live. It looked and felt different here, but this "different" was most desirable and pleasant.

One day, we were drawn to the smell of freshly baked goods and found a small shop. We paused to "inhale" the essence of the locals stopping in to buy their daily must haves. We enjoyed listening to their accents and conversations, taking in their island dress codes and sometimes joining in by chatting with them. We held great, friendly conversations with the locals who were all too eager to learn about life in the USA.

We felt like kids in a candy store, delighting in many of their delicious pastries and freshly squeezed local fruit juices. They had the tastiest and yummiest beef pies, currants rolls and guava cakes, While I was eating a coconut cake, I felt the need to sit for a while to take in the "moments" that I deserved to enjoy the pleasure of its flavor! It was Heavenly, tasty, full of flavor, yummy and oh so delish!

One of the dishes that we both enjoyed immensely was their coconut dumplings. It was served with stewed chicken and various local vegetables. While we ate, I simply closed my eyes and became lost in the moments as I savored every bite. One night, we found this rather small restaurant where we enjoyed their stewed fish that was fried and then topped with a very tasty, spicy, and flavorful sauce made from carrots, onions, and red bell peppers. This dish was washed down with glasses of their delicious and refreshing rum punch. We knew that we had to have more of this punch, and we satisfied our need by returning occasionally to indulge in another cold glass of this delicious drink.

I believe that some countries should not strive to be like the western world, there is much delight in being different. I enjoyed my stay in these islands and would love to revisit if I can.

In February 2020 Art and I, along with our German friends who two years ago hosted us in Munich, went on the 11-day Panama Canal cruise and thoroughly loved our visits to the following countries:

Aruba and Curacao—Visiting these small Dutch desert-like islands reminded me of the landscapes of our very own Arizona but lacking the island character. I enjoyed their funchi, which is a side dish made from cornmeal with a slightly sweet flavor. It is fried and can be shaped to resemble french fries. Their clean, powdery, white-sandy beaches and boldly painted colorful buildings reminded us that we were on an island.

Colombia—The walled city called Cartagena seemed to thrive with bougainvillea plants. These plants, bushes, and trees exploded in such vivid colors everywhere I looked. I enjoyed their local fruits such as the tasty sapodillas and relished in the local pastry shops. I had to have a second helping of their tasty meat pies and the pastelitos, mostly the guava and coconut flavors. I especially delighted in discovering the true diversity of the locals. It is different from the way that this country is portrayed in TV shows and movies. It simply does not reflect their true, wonderful, and vibrant ethnic mix. I took pleasure in discovering the many different race classifications of this country.

Costa Rica—The first stop of our tour was at a fruit and vegetable stand that also housed a gift shop. Here we delighted in drinking some coconut water from a vendor who skillfully chopped open the coconuts with her machete. Fresh pineapple, papaya, sapodilla and other tropical fruits were available for sampling. Their vibrant and calm scenery caused me to be lost in the moments as I smiled at the familiarity of it all. I was able to revisit moments from my own island as I recognized many of the fruit trees and tropical plants such as breadfruit, papaya, cassava, mango, and soursop.

Our next stop was at one of their popular beaches that housed a restaurant. I allowed myself to be immediately distracted by the aroma of the food. I had to have the escovitched fish with rice and peas, various types of steamed vegetables, a small salad, and my all-time favorite—fried plantains. Oh yes, food for the soul. My mood was good before I got there, but it became even better.

Panama Canal—Before I left for the cruise, I did some research on the canal to learn about the history about this century-old wonder. It was constructed to reduce the time for us to get from one ocean to the other. This port was the most anticipated one of our entire cruise.

The truth is it did not fail to please. Being in its presence gave me a much better sense of appreciation and gratification for this unbelievable wonder. When the canal made its debut, I was filled with a mixture of excitement, appreciation, deep respect, and spirituality as I gazed upon the glory of this engineering phenomenon. I quickly became lost in my own thoughts as I tried, without much success, to imagine the numerous challenges they faced by building this lengthy waterway. I also tried to imagine the impact of the thousands of lives that were lost due to diseases such as malaria, measles, and yellow fever.

A visit to this country should be on everyone's bucket list at some point in their lives because some things are better seen than described.

Our visit to a tribal village began with a fun boat ride along a river. When we arrived, while we were climbing up a semi-steep bank, we were melodiously greeted by a group of men of various ages. They played their traditional music using a handmade flute accompanied by different shaped maracas and some small drums. In addition to the musicians, a group of women and small children were on the other side of the riverbank and happily guided us to their community hut. We learned about some aspects of their culture, traditions, language and meanings of their tribal body paintings. They have managed to hold on to ancestral teachings, thus allowing them to live as they prefer on the same lands they knew.

They demonstrated some of their traditional dances that were a ceremonial custom signifying hospitality and friendship. We were honored when they graciously allowed us the opportunity to join in as their partners. We witnessed a traditional performance by the chief of their village. He demonstrated their strong relationship with the earth by granting it full respect. He spoke about always being at risk of forced displacement and cultural extinction.

Their small, elevated homes were brimming with age-old customs and history. They did not have windows or doors. They had very narrow, wooden steps that led up to their huts, which had various sizes of hammocks. They have inherited and preserved their language and culture from the generations who came before and without any doubt, they seek to keep their heritage and legacy alive.

We admired the spectacular and uniquely hand-crafted products that they designed and handcrafted to sell, thus generating a basic means of income. I particularly loved their unique and almost sacred styles of carved statues that somehow gave me the sense that they were transmitting valuable messages to us.

Their baskets were weaved mostly from natural products that they harvested such as strips of bark, certain tree roots and even palm branches. Some of those materials were dyed and layered into the natural colors, thus creating amazing colorful patterns that have cultural meanings and ancestral symbolisms. Some of these baskets symbolize various gods and have specific purposes to store food, clothing, and even liquids. They choose to hold on to these beautiful traditional masterpieces that their ancestors taught them and remain committed about passing on these skills to their younger generations.

Many of the tribes do not get government financial assistance so self-provisions are an everyday objective. They sustain themselves by farming, hunting, fishing, and even producing clothing materials made from natural grasses and trees. The vivid tropical and stunning island-style wraps that the women wore appealed to my Caribbean taste and lifestyle. The colors were superbly bold, happy, and intense.

This visit enhanced my cultural experiences and is a prized add-on. I learned how they valued the land by using every natural resource for the survival of their community. Here, there's a collective sense of belonging, signifying that in some ways they're happier than most of us.

My Social Commentary

It is my greatest wish, hope, and prayer that my story would be able to elevate, encourage, and resonate as a "Me too" story.

In my earlier years, I experienced people who have tried to pull me back into old and familiar patterns of behavior. Finding that inner strength to resist, requires a lot of effort but taking the appropriate action at the right time is so exhilarating. When we put an end to previous lifestyles that no longer compliment us, it is one of life's great accomplishments. Many ends make great and successful beginnings of a new life.

I grew in my consciousness that some of our friends can be so shallow and heartless. At first it can be a shock to our system but finding the courage to move forward and count it as life experiences is an absolute requirement. I believe that when people try to throw their bricks at you, those very bricks should be used to position your own foundation.

❧

Many people seem to enjoy griping about any and everything. They're chronically miserable and stressed but very few of them want to put in the work to escape those mentally troubling states. So much of what we think we need to be happy—a "vaycay," bigger home, new romance, BMW, enhanced lips/butts—make little to no impact on our overall life satisfaction. I like to refer to such idle "wants" as temporary, often materialistic goals. Most of us are already blessed with what we really need but become too busy and selfish to even absorb this truth.

A lot of people live as if money is more important than anything else. The chase for more, causes us to become consumed and easily caught up desperately trying to keep up with society. It is as if we are living in a world where everyone is striving for more and more possessions that are not worth having.

❧

We find ourselves losing many countless and precious moments by finding fault in our spouses, friends, a design, a child, and even someone's opinion. As a result of this oversight, we fail to see the presence of any good that's right in our midst, and consequently miss out on the valuable benefits when it's too late.

Often relationships break up simply because their small problems were left unattended and allowed to fester resulting in bitterness and the settling of scores mindsets. When our egos are wounded our actions may plunge into dangerous and irreversible levels of rationale. Disappointment in the ones closest to you is a hurtful thing. It's crushing and infuriating. It can lead to resentment that ultimately may have a one-way-ticket price tag.

Many people I know, live in an altered state of reality by loving men who are simply making fools of them. They live day by day trying so hard to do the right thing for them. They usually end up getting criticized and blamed because their state of reality is spot-on and different from the wrong and insulting ideas of their partners.

Relationships like this might fail because one partner likes the other more than the other partner likes themselves.

When these foolish partners do not get it, these women need to stop participating in their lies and altered egos. But all too often, without re-alizing that their needs are more important, sadly they choose to stay in those negative spaces. This happens too often because either they are scared to be alone, believe that they would never be understood or that they just don't matter. Staying neutral while their negative attitude rages on and then becomes physically abusive, is like standing in sinking sand.

Women should not tolerate abuse on any level especially if they are stained by violent arguments due to alcoholism, drugs or other factors. Abuse to anyone is degrading, brutal and shocking to even acknowledge. Anger has many ways of finding a way out particularly if it's being suppressed. Those are unsafe spaces to dwell in. For reasons unknown, their partners seem to have no idea that they're even experiencing abuse. We all have different perspectives and expectations and regrettably we might just not be right for each other. Standing up and facing our fears gives us extreme liberation.

Apologies without changed behavior is huge manipulation in my book! I was taught that physical damage can be redressed but moral damage in most cases can be irreparable.

ᏇᏉ

Most of us choose to spend countless hours distracted by our phones rather than becoming enriched in nearby nature activities, and tasks that are meaningful and have virtuous substance.

We seem to be chasing the desire for recognition, wealth, and power. We're constantly counting the number of "likes" that we receive on social media and who is "liking" them. Sadly, we become happy when we see the names of those people who submitted the "likes." What they don't realize is that those "likes" could really be mindless and untrue actions.

Their lives seem to hinge on how many Facebook likes they get, etc. It seems like they are always looking for that feedback to validate whatever they're doing. It also seems to me like they are constantly endorsing or promoting themselves.

Could it be that social media is sought out by lonely people who have the need to feel surrounded by people? As humans, one of our deepest needs is being loved and because of this, we could unquestionably become visibly terrified about people "not liking" us. These types of behaviors may seem to mimic borderline obsession.

I must say though, that we have allowed modern technologies to take us away from the simplicities of life when we were always present and aware of each other. I believe that we are called human beings for a reason, but we are losing the human part of it in our current tech age—internet, Facebook, social media. It serves its purpose, but it can very easily be taken out of context and thus abused. Our attention is under siege by various tech devices particularly our phones that continue to seduce us. We have allowed them to steal the time that we used to connect with people and family and sadly we're missing out on some valuable lessons.

I have observed friends, family members and parents who are constantly missing out on the look of joy/pain in their child's eyes because they are so fixed on Facebook or some other form of social media. It saddens me when I observe people who seem to be in a war for attention. They ignore what their child is trying to tell them because they are so engrossed in their phones. How did we lose the good that was given us? In sharp contrast to those days, nowadays we simply don't care. We don't seem to want to know anything about our neighbors, co-workers, church members or offer to help even when we're made aware of their need.

We have also become a self-centered society because we seem to be continuously competing against each other. Years ago, we had a better sense of the small self and what values we stood for. We seem to have become scattered and careless by allowing basic values to slip away.

☙

In our current world, we are facing blatant divisiveness, racism, and plenty of meanness. As it unfolds, we must look for the light, even in the cracks to give us the courage to act accordingly when we feel attacked unfairly. It irks me to my very core when people of that other race act like and believe that they are better than us—NO they're not! They do not have the right to dominate me or others—I am just as good as them.

During our journeys, we have been subjected to blatant racism many times. This may be because those "other" folks were either raised (or still choose) to believe that they are the chosen race and are superior to any other humans. One evening, Art and I were strolling along the sidewalk by the beach after having had an enjoyable dinner. A jeep with four young men of that other race, slowly drove past us yelling: "Niggers go back where you come from." It's earth-shattering when this occurs but there's little else one can do but just ignore those folks.

On another occasion, we had just purchased our home and were so overjoyed at our new ownership that we returned to the house to celebrate. We removed the For Sale sign and were on our driveway with our sons, who were five and seven at that time, ecstatically speaking with one of our neighbors. Once again, a truck with two young men of the other race drove by. They turned around and threw two beer bottles at us. The bottles smashed as they hit the driveway right in front of our sons, fortunately missing them!

Those acts spoke deep volumes of inhumanity and stupidity. To say what emotions these insane actions conjure up is probably an impossible act to accomplish. This hostile type of behavior is only befitting for trashy folks who possess and execute a sick mentality, and this is wholly not acceptable!

☙

I choose to avoid watching the news channels because I know what I need to exclude from my world. Negativity from it will not steal my joy by gate-crashing into my world. Most times, it's so full of negativity that it all seems like a lot of useless "noise" to me. I see the headlines on my phone and that gives me a good sense of what's current and that's all I need. My time is more valuable than needing to know gory details of the senseless killings and unpleasant political nonsense. This sick political arena in our beloved country is riddled with nonsensical lies and fake appearances. When politicians visit, they tell lies by telling us that they really care about us by shaking our hands, smiling, etc. Yeah right! Some months after they have secured the office, they walk right by without recognizing who you are or care to even know.

One of the things that I have learned over time is how to be quiet and to be in the moment. It's necessary to leave those impersonal streets and activities behind and step inside our front door, closing it firmly behind us as we reclaim the sacred spaces of each other. While I am in the shower I try to take in the fragrance and touch of the soap against my body. I focus on the feel of the scrubbing on my skin followed by the tingling of the water while it's rinsing. I have learned how to reduce distractions by enjoying the scrubbing, smells, the washing and even the bubbles. Sometimes it's in these wonderful and calm moments that my path becomes clear and I find answers to questions that I may have needed.

CURRENT EVENTS

Around December 2019, a virus called COVID-19 was birthed abroad and eventually spread to the US. By March 2020, we were facing serious situations around the world, causing some countries to shut down to inhibit the spread. Not many countries are exempt from the dangers that it has caused. This deadly virus has already caused millions of lives to be lost globally as well as nationwide and the numbers keep rising daily. Vaccines to combat this virus have now been discovered and aggressive attempts are being made to vaccinate our entire country.

We have learned new methods of quarantining ourselves and our families. We have become cognizant of washing our hands frequently, conscious of the signs and symptoms, staying at home and socially distancing ourselves. Wearing masks is mandatory in public places and using gloves while we're shopping, pumping gas, etc., has become the daily norm. It is a new lifestyle that's very different from what we were used to, and one can only hope that very soon what we knew as normal will re-occur. But then again it makes one wonder what the "new" normal would be.

In lieu of using cash, writing checks or swiping our credit cards at a card payment terminal, they have developed ways to provide contactless payments. Some of our credit cards now have a "wave-like" symbol on them that allow us to simply pass the "wave" symbol over the payment terminal without touching it.

COVID-19 has allowed us to engage in new habits of thinking that give us a greater purpose. We have been able to pause and challenge ourselves with different platforms that counteract some of the daily negativity of our changed environments. The impact of this virus has resulted in countrywide layoffs and many businesses closing their doors. For the first time, many companies have had their employees working virtually from their homes. Some schools have closed their doors and provided children with laptops to be taught from their homes. Basically, many homes have been made to endure transformations into offices and schools.

Rather than complain about our new circumstances, we must be willing to adapt and accept what is, without judgment. We need to redefine the new normal and see it as "different." Recently we took a ride down the main street of our lovely little town. People seemed to have chosen to become complacent and are ignoring all warnings about wearing face masks and social distancing themselves. Except for about four people, everyone else were not wearing masks. They were in crowded restaurants at tables that were at normal proximity to each other.

Because of COVID 19, we have had to socially distance ourselves from each other, but reality says that we have always been socially disconnected in many ways. If you look at churches on Sunday mornings, the racial divide is so apparent. You would think that church should be the one place on this earth where we could all find commonality to worship God—yeah right.

SOCIAL UNREST

We are also faced with a very, very racist situation that occurred where a white police officer was caught on video with his knee pressed firmly on a Black man's neck. Even though this Black man was pleading that he could not breathe, that clearly did not matter to this officer. It is a gross insult and blatant brutality to humanity to treat anyone this way. This type of sick brutality offends the very core of my soul. Who does he think he is to pass judgment that this man's life was less important and relevant than his or his family's? How dare he??????

I am angry, sad, and resent ALL police brutality towards any human being. I cringe when I think about my own two sons who face a huge possibility of being treated unjustly by white police officers. Thanks for the modern technology of cameras included in our phones and other devices. Had it not been for the person who took that video, this incident would have been swept under the carpet once more. History shows that this type of race brutality has happened repeatedly but sadly they were simply brushed aside, or the perpetrators were found not guilty. Periodically, stories emerged about Blacks being mistreated but unfortunately the norm is to ignore them.

We have made such remarkable strides with technology and an immense amount of academic excellence but socially and collectively as individuals, we have become even more divided because of race, color, and social norms. Our country is going through some extremely troubling times. It's scary, ugly, shameful, shocking, and very embarrassing to the world. It's insane how the senseless lack of reform within the police departments have been fueling unnecessary brutality towards black people.

I passionately believe some people think that it is a crime to be Black and over time, develop a frame of mind where they wish to eradicate the entire race!—Really??? It seems as though history has never taught them anything different. The issues of justice, inequality, and blatant prejudice towards Black people is contaminated and so corrupt. This race and inequality war has been amplified lately and must be dealt with by each of us reaching out of our comfort zones.

As hard as I may try, I could never understand how some people choose to attack the dignity of anyone, especially the Black race. We are not less than you; we're human too. We are all God's children, and we did not choose to come into this world being Black or otherwise. We are born into, behave, and move in definitive circles that we didn't choose. We are a melting pot of different cultures and ethnicities or haven't you noticed?

It has illuminated racism that has been in existence in so many cases where Blacks have been wrongfully accused. Some folks seem to get a kick from fanning hatred by stoking the embers, trying to ignite it all again. People—Will you ever learn to get it together by changing your beliefs or are you just content to live with willful ignorance??? This incident has currently caused violent unrest, hatred, outrage, and mayhem across our country. We should never have to tolerate or even think about turning a blind eye to being unfairly excluded and treated so violently in any shape or form. It's a dramatic change of events for the other race to see that we have been fighting for the end of racism a very long time ago, but they just could not or refused to "see."

This reality brought about massive amounts of people of all races. They have been protesting to get a valid and praiseworthy justification for the motive of this brutal and very abusive police officer who seemed to have had very intentional and troubling agendas in mind. It seemed to have awakened the consciousness of many Caucasian people. Normally they would not have paid attention or taken offense at the need for effective justice for every race. It has caused a domino effect of chaos and turmoil in many cities all over the world.

Respect for an individual's freedom has almost been lost by the wayside. Instead of peace that brings about prosperity for everyone, some tyrants choose to trample on innocent mankind and should not be allowed to use the law as they wish to interpret it! It is an insane concept to not accept the rule of law. Certain groups of people seem to be the chosen ones and are highly valued over others.

For us to be able to continually develop into a meaningful sense of sanity, we must avoid this deliberate destruction of our development as a people. It is surely leading us down some very uncontrollable paths and will not help to provide racial stability for our future generations. It is real, people, it's not a joke. Just because you were raised in a "privileged" environment and have never had to deal with unfair, unjust, blatant and deliberate, in-your-face racism doesn't mean it doesn't exist!!!

This stuff is real, and we are not making it up!!! It's time to cut this out!!! ENOUGH already! When will this blatant hatred and intolerance be obliterated? What is this compulsion that convinces some people to engage in killing Blacks? When will this hatred be replaced by humans really loving and caring for other humans? When? When?

Honestly, I choose to maintain an incredibly positive vibe in my life. I have always tried my best to be optimistic, but I've lost all hope that racism will ever die the death that it so richly deserves. It is appalling to watch the looting and destruction of people's property.

These acts have occurred by people who have ulterior motives that have little to do with the dire circumstances. Some are angry, hurt, fed-up, disappointed, and tried to find ways to lash back at the offenders. Could it be that some may not have had a stable, reliable foundation required in good family support to draw from? Without that, it gives rise to shameless and despicable ways of surviving unfortunate occurrences.

Today, we strive to live peacefully amongst friends, neighbors, and our families whose political views we detest. Although we may passionately disagree with each other, we need to still encourage one another to share their views. We all need to attempt to walk down that "long" road to find each other. We can then create a common intention on reshaping the world with the common goal of wiping out racism.

We need to be looking for and not away from each other. We are all equipped with unique skills that are not meant to be hidden but to enhance each other's lifestyles. We need to learn how to love, tolerate, and be more compassionate with each other.

All that is born out of darkness will get its judgment in the daylight one day. Systemic racism must one day be totally eradicated. Until such time when we are ALL FULLY onboard with a mindset that fosters more positive changes and a direct intention to do so, then I am afraid it will become just another day!

ARTHUR

I have realized that I was GIVEN Arthur and I became whole—not perfect, but who is? In him, I have a strong emotional connection where I find my place of safety and peace. He gave me free reign to grow, while I defined myself by my ethics and values. In him I find purpose, balance, truth, a passion for life, kindness, a willingness to commit, and the distinct feeling like I am "at home."

During our many years together, I have learned that he's a man of true and immense character who lights up my world. He is my oxygen and I've never felt so alive. He holds a special space for me where I have been able to become whole. He birthed a safe space that allowed me to thrive and know that I am worthy of his love. He has a good head for business and a mature level of common sense. He has a mature and pragmatic way of analyzing things, and I love his creative sense when he suggests alternative solutions. He has embedded in him an endless river of love that flows like a gentle, soothing breeze and ever so selfishly I claim it.

I instantly detected that his precious love was speaking to my deeper self that was unknowingly awaiting and beckoning for him. Because it all made sense, I stepped into his heart then, and even today this amazing unselfish love continues to flow through me. To receive it, I had to make myself available for his version of true love.

My husband, Sgt. Arthur L. Brown served in the Vietnam war from January 1968 through January 1979. He has received numerous medals for his service, including the Bronze Star. Despite having faced many adversities amidst such hostile and unpleasant times, he's the most gentle and caring soul you would ever want to meet. It's a fervent testament of the solid morals and values that he learned from his family. I have thanked God so many times for having kept him safe and sustaining his generous humanity. Throughout our years together, I have always worn this

TRUTH with the fullest pride. About twenty years ago, we were able to reconnect with one of his Army buddies. Two months later, he flew to Ft. Lauderdale to meet up with Art and me. What a homecoming that was! When we had some alone time, Bill told me: Pam, your husband was a saint—in the bush and the trenches of Vietnam!

One of my breathing spaces is having a cup of coffee while I am reading the weekend newspaper. Art shows up just for me even though he does not drink coffee! Over the many years, we have stepped up and out of our humble beginnings. We have received and surrendered our all, to understand and hold on to our unique type of love. He is emotionally and academically intelligent and always tunes in to me to know how I am feeling.

When something is really bothering me, he has this magical way of seeing where my thought process would go in a way that would not be helpful. When I get upset, he stays calm. In my weak and "ruffled" moments, when Art observes how I am reacting to a situation, he helps me function not out of fear but out of love. On days when I may have had a rough day at work and was feeling out of sorts, I anxiously awaited his return home. One look at him, and all those feelings simply melted away. It's not that I cannot live without him, (which truthfully, I can't) it's just that I don't want to.

He excels in managing his emotions and is absorbed in everything that we do because he pays attention. He is confident and profound in the way he thinks and possesses strength in his methods of giving love. We are content with what we have which accounts for our chemistry. He is the delight of my life.

Many years ago, Art took our family to dinner at a restaurant owned by a Trinidadian friend. As a surprise, Art invited two couples who were friends of ours to join us. We had visited there several times before and we loved his homemade soups, but I always teased him that soup isn't soup without dumplings. In the islands it's a standard thing that dumplings are a routine ingredient of soups. I guess he had to modify his soup recipe to please the genre of his customers.

While we were chit chatting, I saw Arthur Jr. coming from the kitchen with a small soup bowl. It was covered by a napkin and he placed it in front of me. I immediately got excited because I thought that the owner had finally included dumplings in the soup—just for me. When I removed the napkin, I saw a small box in the bowl. In the box was the most beautiful diamond ring.

Our friends and I were surprised, and a buzz of excitement emitted from our table. When the owner came out to see us, they all began clapping. Many of the other customers got wind of what was happening at our table and they too began to clap. The owner then switched on his stereo and played that beautiful song most of us may remember—"Endless Love" made popular many years ago by Lionel Richie and Diana Ross. All our friends, as well as the other customers, began beckoning us to dance. They would not let up. So here were Arthur and I in the middle of this lovely restaurant, slow dancing to that delightful song! It has been one of the most memorable and festive nights of our marriage.

On the way home, he told me that he had always wanted to buy me a ring with a genuinely nice diamond. He had discussed the idea with a friend at work who advised him that he should follow his heart and do so. Art had received a substantial award from his job as a bonus for a special project that he had just completed. He used that bonus to buy my beautiful ring. I also learned that during his search, he took our sons with him to several stores searching for the best diamond setting for his wife. I was enormously proud of them all for being able to keep the secret from me. I opened my heart to the whole of it and saw life's many gifts show themselves in so many ways. I had to pay attention to what I have and not get distracted or annoyed over minor elements. He has taught me that he believed in caring for and prioritizing our family. He holds the deepest respect for women and children and is easily troubled if women are excluded, abused, or humiliated.

I believe that Arthur is the missing piece of me because I saw my completion in him. He is a man of honor, love, and understanding. Our lives went from ordinary to extraordinary while we breathed through it. I easily found all that I had deemed as my "imperfections," accepted them and kicked them out of my own self-made cage. I opened myself to his true love, received it, and became a better person for it.

He does not just exist; he is present, and radiates a connection that I fully and joyfully embrace. Every day, I feel totally surrounded by him because he constantly reaches out for all of me. It is an honor to be able to voice these truths about this life that I have shared with him because it's a precious and relentless exactness.

This rhythm of life that we are living is beyond my comprehension. Because he loves me so intensely and is so deeply committed to our family, it gives me purpose and absolutely makes me come alive. I am so enjoying who I have become in this sublime process of learning true love, joy, and excellence. I was already flying but I needed his unique set of wings and discovered that what life has in store for us may be different from what we have in mind.

He has an unfathomable gift of love that I believe by meeting me he truly discovered and learned how to masterfully use it. He is my rock. Our discussions wrap me in an innermost calmness as no one else could. I feel that I am deeply understood, truly supported, utterly loved and I have been living a life resting my head on his gentle shoulders.

He—unlike others—did not think that I needed to be fixed. Because he loves me, I have everything I need. Love is perfect—I met Art.

Our story has been one of the best-laid plans ever and I know for sure that it was definitely not laid out by either of us. This journey has been and still is a pleasure. I believe that he uses his parents, his siblings, and his humble upbringing as the lens through which he views everything. We have kept our feet on the ground—fully grounded, focused and "staying in our lane." We have tried to practice accepting what we have been given, rather than continually asking for more. He has the utmost faith, patience, virtue, self-control, kindness, and respect for everyone.

I admire how nicely he relishes in people's sacred spaces by eagerly attending and actively participating in cultural events way outside of his culture. I am having the life I wanted, needed, and most certainly deserved and I am not afraid of the fact that I'm so very happy.

I have been content in my journey, being careful who I let into my inner circle. I found ways to distance myself from the downbeat ones. This enabled me to come across the true people who have staying power and who are valuable assets to me. My life's destiny will not be compromised by negative beings who never seem to change. If I did not make some hard choices, I would have undoubtedly missed my destiny.

Currently In our daily lives, we crave a simplistic lifestyle focusing mostly on each other's needs. I have found new tenderness, love, patience, and a significant amount of thoughtfulness.

My life is so much richer than what it was. I am present and thankful for the grandeur of everyday. I try not to take a lot of things for granted, having learned that life is a huge collection of moments and the idea is to have and cherish as many as we can. There is no such thing as tomorrow or yesterday. The only real thing is this moment.

Arthur knew love, he taught me love, we have lived love, and my extreme joy continues.

Arthur performing Honor guard duties at a military funeral in 1969

Arthur in Vietnam 1968–69

ABOUT THE AUTHOR

Pamela J. Brown, also known in high school as Jacqueline Abraham, was born on the island of Trinidad, where she graduated from St Joseph's Convent, St Joseph. In January 1971, she pursued her post-secondary studies in Sussex and London, England, where she obtained two registered nursing degrees. She left England in 1978 for the United States, where she started a new career teaching computer software at EDS for two years. She relocated to Florida in 1989 with her family and was employed at Florida Atlantic University. She is now retired and resides there with her husband, Arthur; sons, Arthur Jr. and Richard; daughters-in-law, Janelle and Crystal; and her two grandchildren, Caulen and Kayleigh.